CONT

i

1. An activists' toolkit

"In Amnesty International's experience, violations of human rights and international humanitarian law invariably accompany resort to military force."

Letter from Irene Khan, General Secretary of Amnesty International, to the UN Security Council, October 2002

"Implementation is hampered by continuing inattention to human rights at the national level. Human rights principles, particularly CEDAW [the Convention on the Elimination of All Forms of Discrimination against Women], are frequently not incorporated into domestic law. There is also a lack of knowledge of human rights and legal rights, and limited human rights or legal literacy education. The women whose work is reflected in this study are bringing about change. Their experience and needs form the basis of the link between the local to the global and the global to the local. In so doing, women are transforming the CEDAW into a truly living instrument through being active in this work."

International Women's Rights Project, *The First CEDAW Impact Study*[1]

This report sets out the extent of the legal responsibilities that states, armed groups and individuals have under international law to respect and ensure the rights of women in armed conflict. It encompasses both conflict and post-conflict situations. The emphasis is on state and armed group obligations in relation to violence against women in war,[2] although related abuses by other actors are also addressed.

This report should be read in conjunction with its companion report *Making rights a reality. The duty of states to address violence against women* (AI Index: ACT 77/049/2004), which addresses domestic violence, violence in the community, relevant criminal law and appropriate remedies for victims and survivors of violence against women. States have a duty to ensure women's right to freedom from violence no matter what the context – war or peace, the home, the street or the workplace – and regardless of the identity of the perpetrator – parent, husband, partner, colleague, stranger, police officer, combatant or soldier.

Over the past 10 years, international law in various areas has addressed itself to the worldwide phenomenon of violence against women. This has resulted in a complex legal framework. For example, this report and its companion report cover similar acts (for example, rape) in different situations (war and peacetime) by applying some shared and some distinct legal principles.

Law – whether international or national – consists of a variety of specialized branches. Different rules may apply in different kinds of situations, depending on a variety of factors. These include the legal status of the parties involved and the particular circumstances. For example, a state may assume specific responsibilities by agreeing to be bound by a treaty. This in turn may create obligations – and rights – for certain categories of individuals within that state or in its effective control.

The law alone is not enough to protect women from violence. Given the gap between standards on women's rights and the reality on the ground, ensuring that the law is respected and implemented requires the hard work and advocacy of those who are committed to ensuring that violence is not inflicted on women.

Under international human rights law, states – national governments – bear the primary responsibility for making rights a reality. The key aim of this report and its companion report is to help advocates use international law to press governments to implement their obligations in good faith and in full. Furthermore, armed groups and others involved in armed conflict must also be put under pressure to live up to international standards prohibiting violence against women in war.

The law is a tool – states, armed groups and individuals are obliged to respect the law. Advocates for women's equality can use this tool to remind states that fulfilling women's demands for a life free from violence is not negotiable or discretionary: the state is required to ensure women's right to freedom from violence. They may also use the law as a tool in their work to influence other target groups, such as local communities or members of armed groups.

Radhika Coomaraswamy, the first UN Special Rapporteur on violence against women, its causes and consequences, has pointed out that the legal framework to end violence against women is now in place. The problem is that those with power to secure such a transformation in women's lives are not taking action. They must be challenged, goaded, pressed and inspired to fulfil their obligations in practice.

This toolkit from Amnesty International is a guide to activists and those with influence over public services and policies. These include women survivors of violence, human rights organizations, providers of services to women victims of violence, lawyers, medical professionals, school teachers, academics, social workers, statisticians, police officers, army officers, judges and many more. The toolkit aims to guide them on women's rights under international law, so that they can challenge states to make rights a reality for women.

This can be done through a variety of techniques, which are described in the advocacy report of this toolkit, *Making rights a reality: Campaigning to stop violence against women* (AI Index: ACT 77/052/2004). These techniques include:

▶ lobbying parliamentarians to change the law

▶ pressing ministries and local authorities to improve services, particularly emergency and long-term housing, medical care, and social support, to help women to escape violent situations, to secure justice, and to recover following abuse

▶ bringing challenges to court on the authorities' failure to secure rights for women in practice

▶ harnessing the media to promote progressive messages about women's rights

▶ discussing the causes and costs of violence against women in local communities, and advocating solutions, addressing both men and women

2. Violence against women in armed conflict

Violence against women: definition

The UN Declaration on the Elimination of Violence against Women states in Article 1:

"the term 'violence against women' means any act of gender-based violence that results in, or is likely to result in, physical, sexual or psychological harm or suffering to women, including threats of such acts, coercion or arbitrary deprivation of liberty, whether occurring in public or in private life." [3]

It states in Article 2:

"Violence against women shall be understood to encompass, but not be limited to, the following:

(a) Physical, sexual and psychological violence occurring in the family, including battering, sexual abuse of female children in the household, dowry-related violence, marital rape, female genital mutilation and other traditional practices harmful to women, non-spousal violence and violence related to exploitation;

(b) Physical, sexual and psychological violence occurring within the general community, including rape, sexual abuse, sexual harassment and intimidation at work, in educational institutions and elsewhere, trafficking in women and forced prostitution;

(c) Physical, sexual and psychological violence perpetrated or condoned by the State, wherever it occurs."

In the view of the Committee on the Elimination of Discrimination against Women (CEDAW Committee),

"gender-based violence... is... violence that is directed against a woman because she is a woman or that affects women disproportionately".[4] Further explanation is provided by the NGO Reproductive Health for Refugees Consortium, according to which gender-based violence "encompasses a range of acts of violence committed against females because they are females and against males because they are males, based on how a particular society assigns and views roles and expectations for these people. It includes sexual violence, intimate partner or spouse abuse (domestic violence), emotional and psychological abuse, sex trafficking, forced prostitution, sexual exploitation, sexual harassment, harmful traditional practices... and discriminatory practices based on gender."[5] While some abuses such as forced pregnancy may only happen to women, the fact that an abuse like rape may also happen to men, although with less frequency, does not contradict its gender-based nature.

A worldwide problem

The international community has formally acknow-ledged, in UN Security Council Resolution 1325, that "civilians, particularly women and children, account for the vast majority of those adversely affected by armed conflict, including as refugees and internally displaced persons, and increasingly are targeted by combatants and armed elements".[6] Violence against women in war is widespread, often systematic, and heinous. Reports come from all regions of the world and from a variety of sources.

Africa

"At a far corner of the camp, next to a ditch, a young mother of newborn twins sat in front of a makeshift hut of twigs and cloth. She looked about 17... She had one tiny baby lying on her legs and another at her left breast. Her right breast was swollen to the size of a basketball. Her eyes teared up and she grimaced with pain when she touched it. Her husband explained that she had given birth to the twins a week before, just as they arrived in the camp; she now had a breast infection and her milk was contaminated... 'We need antibiotics, but we have no money and no way to get to the town even if we could buy medicine. There is no transport and they won't let us past the checkpoint.'"[7]

Americas

"...a group of between six and ten military personnel with their faces concealed by black ski masks showed up at the Mejía's house again. One of them – the one who had been in charge of the abduction of (Mr. Mejía) – went into the house... and told her she was also considered a subversive... Mrs. Mejía tried to explain to him that neither she nor her husband belonged to any subversive movements; however, without listening to her he began to spray himself with her perfumes and finally raped her... About twenty minutes later the same person... dragged her into the room and raped her again. Raquel Mejía spent the rest of the night in a state of terror that the one who had assaulted her would come back and fearing for her safety and for her husband's life."[8]

Asia

"We went back home and we were crying. We couldn't tell anyone or we would be executed. It was so shameful so we dug a deep hole and covered it."[9] One of the former "comfort women" subjected to sexual slavery by the Japanese military during the Second World War, explaining why it took decades before they could speak of what had been done to them.

Europe and Central Asia

"Russian soldiers reportedly raped and killed 23-year-old 'Fira' (not her real name) and her mother-in-law, after capturing the town of Shali. Fira was approximately six months' pregnant at the time of her death. Neighbours heard screams and gunshots coming from the house and later discovered the bodies of the two women. One neighbour 'Malika' (not her real name), saw the victims bodies: 'On her breasts, there were dark blue bruises. There was a strangely square bruise on her shoulder. Near her liver, there were also dark bruises. On her neck, there were teeth marks, and her lips also had teeth marks, like someone had bitten her. She had a little hole on the right side of her head, and a big wound on the left side of her head.'"[10]

Middle East and North Africa

"...the fundamentalist armed groups went back to... what they call zaouj al muta or temporary marriage. So, with this justification, many hundreds of women were taken hostage by the fundamentalist armed groups, especially in the countryside, and subjected to a kind of slavery. They had to cook and were sexually abused." After impregnation, some of these women were murdered.[11]

Forms of abuse against women in conflict

Some of the forms of abuse of women and girls in armed conflict which are most frequently documented are: [12]

Gender-based abuses

- rape
- sexual abuse/assault
- deliberate infection with HIV/AIDS
- pornography
- sexual mutilation
- medical experimentation on women's sexual and reproductive organs
- enslavement/sexual slavery/forced marriages or forced cohabitation
- forced impregnation/forced pregnancy
- discrimination against children born from conflict-related rapes and their mothers
- enforced sterilization
- forced abortion
- strip searching/forced public nudity/sexual humiliation
- forced veiling/forced unveiling
- abuses carried out in front of others (adds to humiliation)
- abuses or threats of abuse against women to torture or coerce male relatives
- birth defects, pregnancy complications, sterility due to exposure to chemical weapons[13] and other toxic[14] or prohibited weapons
- threats to/abduction of children
- gender-based forms of arbitrary detention and de facto arbitrary detention
  - in home – by family or by government decree
  - out of home – by armed groups, in rape camps; in state facilities on account of gender
- trafficking in women and girls
- enforced prostitution
- failure to grant refugee status for gender-based harms

Abuses with a disproportionate impact on women or which may be carried out in gender-specific ways

- unlawful killings/deliberate attacks on civilians
- extrajudicial executions
- abductions, "disappearances" or killings of mothers; abductions of babies

- torture or cruel, inhuman or degrading treatment or punishment (some methods gender-based)
- maiming, wounding
- arbitrary detention (conditions often not suited for women; frequent lack of female guards)
- indiscriminate attacks
- "terrorist" attacks
- use of unlawful weapons
- recruitment of girl child soldiers
- forced recruitment of adult women combatants
- deportation/forced displacement/expulsion
- unfair or summary trials (especially for "collaboration" with enemy)
- forced labour, especially domestic
- impact on women of harm to children and partners

Deprivation of economic, social and cultural rights

- denial/withholding of humanitarian assistance
- lack of food leading to malnutrition (often by custom women eat last; girls are fed last)
- lack of adequate sanitary conditions/supplies, especially during menstruation and breast-feeding
- loss of education, employment (may particularly affect women)
- lack of adequate medical care and rehabilitation, including reproductive and maternal health care
- increasing burden of care responsibilities which in most societies fall disproportionately on women
- "double burdens": women assume new roles in public sphere, but still keep prior tasks and responsibilities
- house destruction/demolition/expropriation
- property destruction/confiscation

Consequent abuse and discrimination

- magnification of underlying abuses by discrimination, for example, unmarriageability or loss of husband after rape or amputation due to landmines
- victims perceived as "fallen", "dishonoured" or "disgraced"
- "shame" to family
- "honour killings"/suicides/self-harm following sexual abuse or rumours of sexual abuse
- impunity for perpetrators of gender-based harms (exacerbated by daily impunity for human rights abuse of women)
- perception of women as "secondary" victims
- discrimination in regards to:
  - protection
  - aid
  - rehabilitation
  - reconstruction
  - reintegration
  - repatriation
  - resettlement
  - compensation
  - accountability processes
  - exacerbated by overlapping/multiple discrimination, such as on grounds of religion, ethnicity, sexuality

Particular categories of women at special risk

Some women may face particular danger in conflict situations due to their social position, age, marital status or other factors. Women may fall into more than one of these categories, and thus face an even greater risk of violence. Such categories include:

- girls
- women and girls of child-bearing age
- wounded and disabled women and girls
- internally displaced and refugee women and girls
- members of ethnic/religious/racial/sexual minorities
- indigenous women
- poor women
- women activists
- migrant women, including migrant women workers
- female relatives of well-known male figures
- elderly women
- mothers; single mothers
- war widows and other widows; wives/widows of the "disappeared" or abducted men
- women in inter-communal marriages/relationships/ families
- orphans
- sex workers
- women in institutions
- women combatants and prisoners of war
- women in detention or internment
- mothers of children born of conflict-related rapes, and girls born after such rapes
- single women

Perpetrators

In time of strife, women face harm at the hands of a wide range of people including state agents, members of armed groups and private individuals. Invading soldiers often commit rape and murder. Many armed groups kidnap women and force them to fight or perform domestic labour. Even those sent to help by the international community, such as aid workers or peacekeepers, have been known to

Amnesty International

sexually harass or abuse women. Furthermore, it must not be overlooked that "ordinary" violence against women and girls, such as domestic violence and child abuse, battering, rape, or female genital mutilation, is frequently exacerbated by the pressures of a conflict situation. Sometimes protection or redress for such harm is less available than usual or completely unobtainable due to the breakdown of law enforcement. In addition, women may be unwilling or unable to cooperate with agents of a state they see as threatening in the context of the conflict.

Some frequently implicated perpetrators:

▶ soldiers (own country)
▶ military and other commanders who order or fail to stop abuses
▶ law enforcement officials
▶ unofficial militias/"death squads"/paramilitaries/other groups allied to, acting with consent or acquiescence of the state
▶ armed groups/non-governmental entities
▶ organized criminal gangs
▶ peacekeepers
▶ non-governmental/UN aid workers (both local and international personnel)
▶ foreign troops involved in conflict/occupying forces
▶ third state foreign forces such as soldiers/border guards/refugee camp guards/ third state civilians
▶ community members
▶ family members

People with responsibility to protect women

Many types of people may commit violence against women in conflict, and a wide range of actors have a responsibility to prevent and punish it. This needs to be borne in mind when developing strategies to combat impunity for such atrocities. As the International Committee of the Red Cross (ICRC) has declared: "Everyone must be made responsible for improving the plight of women in times of conflict."[15]

However, the different actors possess different levels and kinds of responsibility and states remain the primary focus of attention.

Some of the relevant actors are:

States
(executive, judicial, legislative branches; law enforcement, military)

▶ home state
▶ second state(s) involved in conflict
▶ third states:
  ▷ as parties to Geneva Conventions and other multilateral treaties
  ▷ in respect of their obligations to the international community (*erga omnes*)[16]
  ▷ as recipients of asylum-seekers/refugees
  ▷ as aid donors
  ▷ as supporters of involved governments or armed groups

International organizations
▶ UN
▶ international financial institutions
▶ regional organizations

Armed groups
Corporations
Individuals

Key phases

Violence against women occurs at every stage before, during and after conflict. Before full-blown hostilities develop, mounting pressures may increase the incidence of acts of violence against women. In fact, some have suggested that increasing levels of violence against women may be used as a warning sign of armed conflict in prevention and early-warning strategies.[17] Furthermore, the risk of such acts does not end with the close of official military operations: violence against women often continues and is sometimes exacerbated in post-conflict phases.

Therefore, strategies to address violence against women should consider all stages including:

▶ conflict prevention/pre-conflict phase
▶ conflict
▶ flight from conflict
▶ post-conflict

These phases should be seen fluidly rather than in a strictly sequential way. Women frequently face grave harm long before the threshold is met to trigger international law governing conflict. Some have questioned whether it is ever "peacetime" for women, given the ongoing nature of violence against women.[18]

In addition, there are military-related abuses in non-conflict situations. These include discrimination against

6

women in the military, such as relegation to certain jobs with lower pay, prohibitions on same-sex relations, sexual harassment and abuse. They also include soldiers' participation in domestic abuse or attacks on women in the community (especially sexual abuse and gender-based murder) around military bases and barracks.

Military structures and militarization are often seen by feminist scholars as perpetuating gender stereotypes – strong male protectors and weak female population – and discriminatory attitudes which foster violence.[19] The use of force is a particularly gendered activity. One contributory factor is the lack of representation of women in the military and its leadership around the world. There are 23 million soldiers in standing armies around the world, of whom some 97 per cent are male, according to anthropologist Joshua Goldstein. Women serving in armed forces tend to be in administrative or "caring" roles. Combat forces have been estimated as being 99 per cent male, reflecting the widespread notion that women are intrinsically unsuited to such activity. A number of states have made reservations to the Convention on the Elimination of All Forms of Discrimination against Women arguing that the principle of equality in public life does not extend to combat-related duties. Women are under-represented in other forms of political organization as well, including governments and intergovernmental organizations, but the under-representation is most extreme in the military sphere.

Of course, women too can violate human rights during wartime, as the images of US women soldiers taunting and ill-treating Iraqi detainees in Abu Ghraib prison attests. But the lack of women in the military and in command positions and combat roles has particular effects on the behaviour of soldiers and on the lives of the women they encounter. There may also be dire consequences for the women in the societies and communities to which fighters return following combat. Some studies have shown higher levels of domestic violence, sexual assault and even spousal murder in post-combat situations.

Types of strife

The level of public violence in a society is used to classify its current situation and determine which international law is applicable. International humanitarian law distinguishes between "armed conflicts" and "situations of internal disturbances and tensions, such as riots, isolated and sporadic acts of violence and other

acts of a similar nature" which fall below the threshold of armed conflict and to which humanitarian law does not apply.[20]

The conflict status therefore determines which bodies of international law apply. Though internal armed conflict has been the most frequent form of conflict since the end of the Second World War, less international legal protection is available in such situations than in international armed conflicts.

Human rights are often drastically affected by the onset of armed conflict. However, human rights law is still applicable in any situation of emergency, including armed conflicts in all their variations.

Some human rights may never be suspended in any circumstances. However, several international human rights treaties allow states to derogate from (suspend or restrict) certain human rights guarantees in narrowly defined circumstances, such as an emergency threatening the life of the nation, but only to the extent strictly required by the situation.

It should be noted that the relationship between the humanitarian and human rights branches of international law is not always easy to specify. Even in times of internal strife and armed conflict, Amnesty International encourages states and other parties to conflicts to apply the stricter provisions of international human rights law.

The following list sets out which bodies of international law offer protection in the various different types of situation addressed in this report.

Internal disturbance/state of emergency
International human rights law applies, to the extent that it has not been derogated from or is non-derogable (cannot be suspended or restricted).

Internal armed conflict
International human rights law applies, to the extent that it has not been derogated from or is non-derogable. A subset of the provisions of international humanitarian law also applies (see below).

International armed conflict
The full panoply of international humanitarian law applies. Human rights law applies, to the extent that it has not been derogated from or is non-derogable. Some of its provisions, such as the right to life, are interpreted in light of international humanitarian law.

One

3. Relevant bodies of law

A number of bodies of law pertain to women in armed conflict. The first, and most obvious, is national law (what international law calls "municipal law"). That is largely beyond the scope of this report, which focuses on international law, but should not be forgotten. At the international level, two primary bodies of law must be closely studied: international human rights law (both at the universal and regional levels) and international humanitarian law. International humanitarian law applies in addition to international human rights law, supplying further protections given the special circumstances of armed conflict. Some of this international law has been rigorously critiqued by feminist scholars.[21] These criticisms are not discussed at any length in this report, which aims to inform activists as to what legal provisions are currently available. However, they must not be forgotten by activists seeking both to use the law to protect women and to shape the progressive development of the law in the future.

This report also touches on several other related and overlapping areas of international law, including international criminal law, international refugee law and the law on the use of force. Crimes against humanity[22] and genocide[23] are covered by human rights law, war crimes are covered by international humanitarian law. All three are covered by international criminal law.

International law

Classical international law focused almost exclusively on relations between states. International law today governs inter-state relations, but also the relationship between states and those within their effective control and even, in some cases, between individuals. Still, state obligations are most often the frame of reference for all of these matters. However, through international criminal law, increasingly, individuals may be held accountable for violating international law.

Article 38 of the Statute of the International Court of Justice lists the sources of international law. The primary sources are treaties; international custom, as evidence of a general practice accepted as law;[24] and general principles of law.[25] Judicial decisions and the views of the most highly qualified scholars (known as "publicists") are considered supplemental sources.

Comments by human rights treaty bodies, special human rights mechanisms, and the resolutions of international political bodies such as the UN General Assembly and the Security Council may be considered as authoritative interpretations of binding treaty standards or evidence of principles of customary international law.

Certain rules of international law are of such importance that they are accepted as "peremptory norms" from which states may not deviate. They may not be exempt from their obligation to respect these rules under any circumstances. A peremptory norm, also known as a norm of *jus cogens*, is defined in the Vienna Convention on the Law of Treaties, which governs treaties between states, as "a norm accepted and recognized by the international community of states as a whole as a norm from which no derogation is permitted and which can be modified only by a subsequent norm of general international law having the same character."[26]

Treaties are one of the primary sources of international law. Treaties are written agreements between states (or sometimes between states and intergovernmental organizations) governed by international law. A particular treaty is only legally binding on states that choose to adhere to it either by ratifying or acceding to the treaty. This is a sovereign decision, which all states are free to make. Before citing a particular treaty provision, one needs to be certain that the state in question has ratified or acceded to the treaty, or otherwise phrased, is a state party to the treaty. For human rights treaties, this can be checked on the website of the UN High Commissioner for Human Rights.[27]

A treaty provision can acquire the status of customary international law over time, thus binding on all states including non-parties, but the standard for this is very high. Authoritative commentators have indicated that the principle of non-discrimination on the grounds of sex has been identified as a norm of customary international law.[28]

A treaty may be called a treaty, covenant, convention, pact or protocol and these terms have the same legal effect. A protocol is an additional treaty, appended to an underlying treaty. Sometimes only those states that have ratified the underlying treaty may ratify the Protocol thereto. This is the case for the Optional Protocol to the Convention on the Elimination of All Forms of Discrimination against Women. However, in other cases, where the treaty so specifies, states that are not parties to the underlying convention may still become parties to the protocol. The Optional Protocol to the Convention on the Rights of the Child on the involvement of children in armed conflict is one such instrument.

Furthermore, when ratifying a treaty, a state may register a reservation – a statement limiting the scope of the legal responsibilities which it is undertaking.[29] A state is then bound by the treaty, but with some limits on its obligations. Importantly, a reservation must not be counter to the object and purpose of the treaty, according to the Vienna Convention on the Law of Treaties.[30] States have violated this rule with their numerous, sweeping reservations to the Convention on the Elimination of All Forms of Discrimination against Women (CEDAW).

To determine the nature of the international law provisions designed to protect women in time of conflict, this report looks at a range of these sources. However, it focuses largely on treaty law, supplemented by comments by human rights treaty bodies, the resolutions of international political bodies such as the UN General Assembly and Security Council, judicial decisions, and the views of experts in the field. Care needs to be taken when assigning value to these sources, so that the most powerful and unassailable legal case can be built.

International human rights law

International human rights law is a subset of international law. It addresses the rights and dignity of all human beings – women, men and children – without discrimination. It provides that states must respect and protect human rights and ensure that those within their jurisdiction enjoy their human rights in practice. Traditionally it has been seen as applying solely to the relationship between the state and individuals. However, more recently it has been recognized that the state also has a responsibility to intervene when individuals act in ways that affect the rights of others.

Human rights law is drawn from treaties such as CEDAW, and from all other types of source discussed above.

International humanitarian law

International humanitarian law applies in situations of armed conflict – not only international wars between states, but also internal armed conflicts between governments and armed groups, or among armed groups. International humanitarian law applies in addition to international human rights law, supplying further protections given the special circumstances of armed conflict. International humanitarian law lays down standards of conduct for combatants (those taking an active part in hostilities) and their leaders. Broadly it seeks to put limits on the means and methods of warfare (for example, there are rules against the use of indiscriminate weapons, perfidy, abusing signs of truce, or using disproportionate methods of achieving military objectives) and to protect those not taking an active part in hostilities from harm – for example, the sick and wounded, the shipwrecked, prisoners of war and civilians. The obligations of states to address violence against women under international humanitarian law are covered in this report.

International humanitarian law prohibits many acts, specifying that particular breaches of the rules are war crimes, and that all states have an obligation to seek out and bring perpetrators of such crimes to justice. Therefore there is a strong link with international criminal law, another area of law covered in this report.

International criminal law

International criminal law relates to crimes under international law, which may be drawn from treaty (for example, the definition of torture under the UN Convention against Torture), custom (for example, the definition of crimes against humanity until they were codified in the Rome Statute of the International Criminal Court), or international humanitarian law (war crimes, particularly grave breaches of the Geneva Convention and violations of the laws and customs of war).

International criminal law has become particularly pertinent to violence against women over the last 10 years. During this time, the development of definitions of crimes, the jurisprudence of the two ad hoc international criminal tribunals for Rwanda and former Yugoslavia, and the drafting and adoption of the Rome Statute of the International Criminal Court have defined violence against women more thoroughly than ever before in international law, and in a manner which is more gender-sensitive and reflects to a greater extent the victim's experience of violence. The methods of investigation and court procedures of these international tribunals are increasingly sensitive to the needs and safety of witnesses and victims, particularly of sexual violence (although there is still much to be done in this area). They provide an important model of good practice for domestic criminal law systems.

International refugee law

The plight of refugees is fundamentally a human rights issue, and many people become refugees because they are fleeing situations of armed conflict. International refugee law is therefore closely connected to human rights law and international humanitarian law. International refugee law provides protection for people forced to flee their country of origin because they are at risk of human rights abuse.

Part Two: INTERNATIONAL HUMAN RIGHTS LAW

4. Legal obligations of parties to armed conflicts under human rights law

States' legal obligations

States' underlying obligations under human rights law to prevent violence against women are not diminished by the onset of an armed conflict. These obligations are detailed in the companion report *Making rights a reality: The duty of states to address violence against women* (AI Index: ACT 77/049/2004).

In the specific context of armed conflicts, states should criminalize, in their domestic laws, gender-based war crimes, crimes against humanity and persecution. They should ensure that any violations are investigated and suspected perpetrators brought to justice. States should provide fully accessible complaints mechanisms to women victims, and a full remedy, including compensation, as well as restitution, rehabilitation, satisfaction and guarantees of non-repetition.[31] Public information campaigns need to be carried out, in time of peace and in time of conflict and post-conflict. These are to counter stereotypical attitudes which promote war crimes and other conflict-related violence against women, including members of minority groups or other perceived "enemy" women. Gender-sensitive training must be provided for all military personnel and others involved in the conflict. Specialized counselling and support services need to be created and made available for women victims of armed conflict.

Due diligence and violence against women in armed conflicts

States are obliged under international human rights law to exercise "due diligence" for the protection of women's human rights. This is discussed in detail in the companion report.[32]

The essence of this obligation has been summarized by the UN Special Rapporteur on violence against women, its causes and consequences:

"States must promote and protect the human rights of women and exercise due diligence:

(a) To prevent, investigate and punish acts of all forms of VAW [violence against women] whether in the home, the workplace, the community or society, in custody or in situations of armed conflict;

(b) To take all measures to empower women and strengthen their economic independence and to protect and promote the full enjoyment of all rights and fundamental freedoms;

(c) To condemn VAW and not invoke custom, tradition or practices in the name of religion or culture to avoid their obligations to eliminate such violence;

(d) To intensify efforts to develop and/or utilize legislative, educational, social and other measures aimed at the prevention of violence, including the dissemination of information, legal literacy campaigns and the training of legal, judicial and health personnel."[33]

In the context of armed conflicts, this means that states must not only refrain from acts which violate human rights law, but must also take all necessary measures to prevent other actors (enemy forces, armed groups, paramilitaries, organizations and individuals in a woman's community or family) from committing such acts. As the former UN Special Rapporteur on violence against women, Radhika Coomaraswamy stated: "a State that does not act against crimes of violence against women is as guilty as the perpetrators".[34] Where states have failed to prevent such abuse, they must ensure reparations and rehabilitation for survivor-victims, and strive to bring perpetrators to justice, whether nationally or internationally.

The due diligence standard

The due diligence standard is used to measure state compliance with international human rights obligations in other areas, as well, most often involving protecting persons from abuses by private actors. In fact, due diligence has become the primary human rights standard for assessing how a government responds to non-state or private abuses.

Evolving over many years in the law on state responsibility, particularly with regard to the protection of "aliens", the concept crystallized in the 1988 *Velázquez-Rodríguez* case before the Inter-American Court of Human Rights.[35] The court held that an illegal act by a private actor could lead to international legal responsibility of the state if the state failed to exercise "due diligence" to prevent or respond to the violation in question. The factual situation may restrict the scope of this obligation.

Due diligence is about assessing whether a state has "acted with sufficient effort and political will to fulfil its human rights obligations."[36] Meeting this standard requires that states:

▶ ensure that their criminal and civil laws adequately protect women, in theory and practice

▶ ensure that their justice systems consistently hold perpetrators accountable

▶ actively prevent, investigate and punish violations of women's human rights

▶ provide reparations to women victims of human rights violations, including restitution, compensation, rehabilitation, satisfaction and guarantees of non-repetition

The former UN Special Rapporteur on violence against women has written that: "States are under a positive duty to prevent, investigate and punish crimes associated with violence against women." [37]

The due diligence standard means that when a private perpetrator commits an abuse, and the state fails to respond in accordance with law, it thereby is responsible for a human rights violation itself. The Center for Women's Global Leadership noted, "The failure to exercise due diligence constitutes a human rights violation", and it went on to explain that where private perpetrators feel that their abuses are tolerated, the state has failed to meet the due diligence test.[38]

The due diligence standard judges whether states have truly fulfilled their duties to respect and ensure human rights, to translate human rights norms from elegant pieces of paper to concrete and effective action. Has the state made policy choices which are adequate to address the issue? Has it committed sufficient resources to this end?[39]

Responsibilities of armed groups

International law traditionally focused on regulating relations between states; it was quite literally inter-national law. In today's world, the international legal system has been forced to take into account a wide range of other actors including international organizations, individuals, corporations, armed groups and other non-governmental entities. In almost no arena is this more important than with regard to armed conflict, where non-governmental forces and armed groups play a significant role in the perpetration of human rights abuses, including violence against women.

Human right treaties, in a standard analysis, do not address the obligations of armed groups and other non-state actors, which are in any case unable to become formal parties to such agreements. However, some innovative approaches have been developed, by the UN Children's Fund (UNICEF) in particular, to elicit commitments from some armed groups to abide by certain human rights norms, such as the Convention on the Rights of the Child.

Non-treaty standards often speak to the roles and responsibilities of non-state actors directly. The Universal Declaration of Human Rights, for example, declares itself as a standard not only for states, but for "every individual and every organ of society". Other non-treaty standards offer more detailed recommendations regarding the conduct of armed groups.

5. International human rights law: treaties

As described in *Making rights a reality: The duty of states to address violence against women*, the principle that violence against women is a prohibited form of discrimination and that states must exercise due diligence to prevent, investigate and punish it is enshrined in many human rights treaties (including the International Covenant on Civil and Political Rights, through General Comment 28). This treaty principle is therefore binding on almost all states.

Convention on the Elimination of All Forms of Discrimination against Women

The UN Convention on the Elimination of All Forms of Discrimination against Women (CEDAW), adopted in 1979 and a product of the times in which it was drafted, does not use the word "violence" once in its entire text.[40] This treaty sets out the obligations of state parties to combat discrimination and promote substantive equality for women and is the most important human rights treaty focused specifically on women's human rights, so the omission is striking.

General Recommendation 19

The CEDAW Committee, created under CEDAW to monitor its implementation, sought to rectify this situation when, in 1992, it issued the ground-breaking General Recommendation 19.[41] This recommendation states that **gender-based violence *is* a form of discrimination** which gravely affects women's enjoyment of their human rights. (Paragraph 1)

Examples of gender-based violence given in General Recommendation 19 include: "family violence", forced marriage, dowry deaths, acid attacks, "female circumcision", sexual harassment, compulsory sterilization or abortion or conversely denial of reproductive health services, battering, rape and other forms of sexual assault and, in certain circumstances, "the abrogation of... family responsibilities by men". This sort of violence, as a form of discrimination, is then clearly covered by CEDAW itself. In the CEDAW Committee's view, this means that "[t]he full implementation of the Convention required States to take positive measures to eliminate all forms of violence against women." (Paragraph 4)

States must not perpetrate violence against women through their agents. States must also not fail to act with "due diligence to prevent violations of rights or to investigate and punish acts of violence" committed against women by "any person, organization or enterprise" (Paragraph 9). States must also provide compensation for the women involved. Otherwise, they will be in violation of CEDAW and other norms of international law. This clearly includes violence against women in the framework of armed conflict.

The CEDAW Committee takes a broad view of the human rights consequences for women of gender-based violence. The rights implicated include the right to equality in employment, equal access to health care, the rights of rural women and the right of women to decide on the number and spacing of their children. The CEDAW

Committee notes that "[v]iolence against women puts their health and lives at risk". (Paragraph 19)

To end the violence which deprives women of these basic rights, states are responsible, *inter alia*, for working to diffuse traditional stereotyped attitudes towards women and harmful traditional practices based on such prejudices, to protect rural women, and to "suppress ... traffic in women and exploitation of ... prostitution". (Paragraph 13)

With specific reference to armed conflict, General Recommendation 19 makes clear that gender-based violence which impairs or nullifies "the right to equal protection according to humanitarian norms in time of international or internal armed conflict" is prohibited by CEDAW. (Paragraph 7c) Other particularly relevant rights specifically enumerated include the right to life; to be free from torture or cruel, inhuman or degrading treatment or punishment; to liberty and security of the person; and to the highest available standards of physical and mental health.

Article 6 of CEDAW prohibits all forms of traffic in women and "exploitation of prostitution". In reference to this, the Committee states that "Wars, armed conflicts and the occupation of territories often lead to increased prostitution, trafficking in women and sexual assault of women, which require specific protective and punitive measures." (Paragraph 16)

What is the status of General Recommendation 19?
Article 21 of CEDAW specifically allows the CEDAW Committee to make general recommendations based on its work to the UN General Assembly. A General Recommendation may therefore be seen as an authoritative interpretation of CEDAW, a treaty or primary source of international law. CEDAW is binding on all states parties to the Convention of which there were 179 as of 27 October 2004, but is not binding on non-parties. Signatories of CEDAW that have not yet ratified the treaty have the obligation not to defeat the object and purpose of the treaty's provisions, but do not have to implement it in full.[42]

The obligations of states, according to General Recommendation 19
What must states do to "overcome all forms of gender-based violence, whether by private or public act", including in armed conflict, according to General Recommendation 19?

The requirements include:

▶ taking "effective legal measures," such as adequate penal sanctions, civil remedies and compensatory provisions to protect women (Paragraphs 24 a, b, i, r(i), r(ii), t(i))

▶ adopting preventive measures, including public information and education programmes (Paragraphs 24f, g, m, p, t(ii))
▶ undertaking protective measures, including counselling, rehabilitation and support services for women victims and those at risk (Paragraphs 24b, k, r(iii), r(iv), r(v), t(iii))
▶ providing gender-sensitive training for public officials, especially the judiciary and law enforcement (Paragraph 24b)
▶ compiling statistics and carrying out research on violence against women (Paragraph 24c)
▶ promoting respect for women by the media (Paragraph 24d)
▶ organizing education and public information programmes to combat prejudice against women (Paragraphs 24f, t(ii))
▶ enforcing preventive and punitive measures necessary to overcome trafficking and sexual exploitation (Paragraph 24g)
▶ affording effective complaints procedures and remedies, including compensation (Paragraph 24i)
▶ taking measures to "overcome... female circumcision" (Paragraph 24l)

and

▶ ensuring reproductive rights (Paragraph 24 m)
▶ making sure that any steps taken are accessible to rural women and those in isolated communities (Paragraph 24o)
▶ offering training and employment opportunities, and monitoring conditions of domestic workers (Paragraph 24p)
▶ criminalizing all forms of "family violence", and repealing the "defence of honour" (Paragraph 24r(i) and (ii))
▶ making certain that civil remedies, rehabilitation and support services are available in case of domestic violence (Paragraph 24 r - all subparagraphs)
▶ reporting to the CEDAW Committee on all such measures taken and their effectiveness, along with data on the incidence of gender-based violence (Paragraphs 24e, h, j, n, q, s, u and v)

The meaning of General Recommendation 19 in armed conflict
To translate these obligations into the context of an armed conflict, states should criminalize, in their domestic laws, gender-based war crimes, crimes against humanity and persecution. They should ensure that any violations are investigated, with suspected perpetrators brought to justice. They should provide fully accessible complaints

mechanisms to women victims and compensation, whether the abuse occurred at the hands of the state, an armed group or a private individual. Public information campaigns should be undertaken, in time of peace and in time of conflict and post-conflict, to counter stereotypical attitudes which promote war crimes and other conflict-related violence against women, including those labelled as "enemy" women. Gender-sensitive training should be provided for all military personnel and others involved in the conflict. Specialized counselling and support services should be created and made available for women victims of armed conflict. These are just some examples of what states should do to respect their obligations under CEDAW relative to violence against women in armed conflict.

Optional Protocol to CEDAW

The Optional Protocol to CEDAW[43] was adopted in 1999 by the UN General Assembly and strengthens the mandate of the CEDAW Committee.[44] It offers a complaints procedure for individual women or groups of women to petition the Committee about violations of their rights under the Convention by a state party. Under General Recommendation 19, this could clearly include gender-based violence in wartime or post-conflict for which the state is legally responsible. Further, unless a state party declares otherwise on ratification, the Protocol allows the Committee to undertake inquiries or investigations into allegations of systematic violations of CEDAW, such as systematic discrimination, including systematic gender-based violence against women in conflict. This mechanism can be an important tool in creating a strong new jurisprudence of the CEDAW Committee on violence against women in conflict. Women victims should be encouraged to submit cases with regard to the 69 current state parties.[45] States that are parties to CEDAW (required for accession to the Protocol), but that have not ratified the Optional Protocol, should be encouraged as a matter of priority to do so. They should be urged to ratify it without limiting the Committee's recourse to the inquiry procedure.

Convention on the Rights of the Child

The UN Convention on the Rights of the Child (CRC), adopted in 1989, codifies the rights of people below the age of 18.[46] Hence, the rights of girls under the age of 18 must be seen through the prism not only of general human rights law and of CEDAW, but also of the CRC

and its protocols (see below) as well. Indeed the Committee on the Rights of the Child, the relevant treaty monitoring body, has said that the CRC and CEDAW should be seen to "have a complementary and mutually reinforcing nature."[47]

With 192 state parties, including all states in the world except for Somalia and the USA, the CRC is one of the most widely ratified human rights treaties and thus should command great respect.

According to the CRC, girls, like boys, are guaranteed the following rights pertinent to their protection during armed conflict:

▶ non-discrimination on the basis of sex (Article 2)
▶ the right to life (Article 6)
▶ the right to a name and nationality (Article 7)
▶ the right not to be separated from their parents, except in their best interests (Article 9)
▶ the right to assistance with family reunification (Articles 9(4), 10)
▶ the right to leave and enter their own country (Article 10)
▶ the right to enjoyment of the highest attainable standard of health, including rehabilitation (Article 24)
▶ the right to an adequate standard of living, including the right to assistance, if needed (Article 27)

and

▶ the right to education (Article 28).

Article 37 of the CRC sets out many civil and political rights to which children are entitled. Under its provisions, state parties must ensure that children, including girls, are free from:

▶ torture or ill-treatment (Article 37(a))
▶ capital punishment (Article 37(a))
▶ life imprisonment without possibility of parole (Article 37(a))
▶ arbitrary deprivation of liberty (Article 37(b))

and are entitled to:

▶ legal assistance (Article 37d)) and humane treatment (Article 37c) if deprived of liberty in accordance with the law .

They must also be accorded fair trial rights (Article 40) where applicable. Furthermore, state parties must combat the illegal transfer of children abroad (Article 11) and

Two

protect children from all forms of physical or mental violence, injury or abuse, neglect or negligent treatment, maltreatment or exploitation, including sexual abuse. (Article 19) States need to work to prevent such ill-treatment, and to facilitate the reporting of such incidents, investigation of allegations and care for the children involved. Particular focus on sexual abuse and exploitation is to be found in Article 34 which requires states to prevent the exploitation of children for prostitution or pornography. Article 35 requires states to act against a range of abuses, including abduction or trafficking in children for any reason. UNICEF has noted as issues of concern under Article 35: trafficking in children separated from their parents or orphaned by war, including through adoption; and the forced recruitment of children.[48]

Children affected by conflict

Article 38 of the CRC is arguably the single most crucial article of the Convention for the protection of girls from violence in armed conflicts. Article 38 requires states to respect and ensure the guarantees of international humanitarian law applicable to children, to make certain that no one under 15 takes direct part in fighting or is recruited into its armed forces, and to take all "feasible measures" to safeguard children affected by conflict.[49]

This is supplemented by specific protections for refugee children to be found in Article 22. Refugee children are entitled to receive appropriate protection and humanitarian assistance. They are also entitled to assistance in tracing their parents.

According to the UNICEF *Implementation Handbook for the Convention on the Rights of the Child*, the impact of armed conflict on children should be considered in terms of all of the rights in the treaty. Furthermore, the CRC's provisions are, in its view, "not subject to derogation in times of armed conflict."[50] The Committee on the Rights of the Child takes a holistic approach to the issue and urges comprehensive government action. For example, it recommended to the government of war-torn Sierra Leone that it:

"take all necessary measures in cooperation with national and international NGOs and United Nations bodies, such as UNICEF, to address the physical needs of children victims of the armed conflict, in particular child amputees, and the psychological needs of all children affected directly or indirectly by the traumatic experiences of the war. In this regard, the Committee recommends that the State Party develop as quickly as possible a long-term and comprehensive programme of assistance, rehabilitation and reintegration."[51]

Another aspect of the CRC which is vitally important to armed conflict is its innovative provision for the rights of children with disabilities. A girl with a disability is entitled to have her participation in society and her self-reliance promoted and she should be treated with dignity. She has the right to special assistance without charge and to rehabilitation. (Article 23)

In another innovative treaty provision, if a child is a victim of any kind of violence, exploitation or torture, or of an armed conflict, states must take all necessary measures to help the child recover, physically and mentally. (Article 39)

The central principle of the CRC is that the "best interests of the child shall be a primary consideration" in all actions concerning children, whether taken by courts or administrative or legislative bodies. (Article 3) If it were truly applied to decision-making about armed conflict, this principle could be revolutionary, especially when coupled with Article 6(2)'s exhortation that "States Parties shall ensure to the maximum extent possible the survival and development of the child."

Optional Protocol to the Convention on the Rights of the Child on the involvement of children in armed conflict

In the 1990s, after the Convention on the Rights of the Child entered into force, the international community realized that the minimum age for children's participation in armed conflict had been set too young. To rectify this, the Optional Protocol to the Convention on the Rights of the Child on the involvement of children in armed conflict was drafted and later adopted by the UN General Assembly in May 2000.[52] This treaty offers greater protection to teenagers, including girls, from conscription and forced and voluntary recruitment into armed service, and from participation in hostilities. When serving as combatants, girls may be at grave risk of violence, including as prisoners of war or detainees or on the field, or even within their own units.

This Optional Protocol requires state parties to:

▶ take "all feasible measures" to ensure that any members of their armed forces under 18 do not take "direct part in hostilities" (Article 1)
▶ ensure that no one under 18 is compulsorily recruited into their armed forces (Article 2)
▶ raise the minimum age of voluntary recruitment into the armed forces, aiming towards the age of 18; make a binding declaration as to what that age is (Article 3)

Any "voluntary" recruitment of people under the age of 18 must:

▶ be genuinely voluntary
▶ be carried out with the informed consent of the person's parents or guardians
▶ require reliable proof of age

Armed groups not forming part of the forces of the state are not to recruit anyone under 18, voluntarily or otherwise, or to make use of them in hostilities. States are to take "all feasible measures" to prevent such recruitment or use. (Article 4) Any steps taken to implement these rules are to be reported to the Committee on the Rights of the Child. (Article 8)

Optional Protocol to the Convention on the Rights of the Child on the sale of children, child prostitution and child pornography

The Optional Protocol to the Convention on the Rights of the Child on the sale of children, child prostitution and child pornography was adopted in 2000 to address another set of grave issues of concern.[53] Although written largely in gender-neutral terms, its preamble recognizes that "girl children... are at greater risk of sexual exploitation and that girl children are disproportionately represented among the sexually exploited..."

States that adhere to this Protocol must:

▶ prohibit the sale of children
▶ prohibit child prostitution
▶ prohibit child pornography

Such acts are to be criminalized, with those who exploit children in such situations penalized rather than the children themselves, and punished by appropriate penalties.[54] States can exercise jurisdiction over such offences, wherever the perpetrators may be found, (Article 4) and are to cooperate at the international level to combat these abuses. Child victims are to be protected and supported throughout this process and are entitled to compensation and rehabilitation. Education is to be undertaken about the gravity of these types of offences. All measures taken to these ends are to be reported to the Committee on the Rights of the Child.

This protocol could offer great protection for girls in conflict and especially post-conflict situations, when they may be at particular risk of such abuses due to poverty, dislocation and social breakdown.

International Covenant on Civil and Political Rights

The International Covenant on Civil and Political Rights (ICCPR),[55] along with its two Optional Protocols, the International Covenant on Economic, Social and Cultural Rights and the Universal Declaration of Human Rights, together form the International Bill of Human Rights. The International Bill of Human Rights represents the cornerstone of human rights law.

Importantly, this treaty requires state parties to both *respect and ensure* human rights (Article 2) and to do so *without discrimination on the basis of sex*. This means that the state must refrain from violations against women and must also protect women from abuses committed by other actors, whether in peacetime or war.

In the view of the Human Rights Committee, the body set up under the ICCPR to monitor its implementation:

"the positive obligations on States Parties to ensure Covenant rights will only be fully discharged if individuals are protected by the State, not just against violations of Covenant rights by its agents, but also against acts committed by private persons or entities that would impair the enjoyment of Covenant rights..."[56]

According to the Human Rights Committee, states are required by the ICCPR to exercise "due diligence" to both prevent as well as punish, investigate and redress harms committed by non-state actors.[57] In addition, the Human Rights Committee has warned states that justifications for violations of women's human rights on the basis of "traditional," "cultural" or "religious attitudes" are unacceptable.[58]

A number of the ICCPR's provisions are relevant to women in conflict and post-conflict situations. Guaranteed rights in the ICCPR, which may be significant in the context of armed conflict, include:

▶ the right to life (Article 6), which includes a prohibition on the execution of pregnant women (Paragraph 5)
▶ the right to be free from torture; cruel, inhuman or degrading treatment or punishment; and involuntary medical experimentation (Article 7)
▶ the right to be free from slavery and servitude (Article 8)
▶ the right to liberty and security of the person; the right to be free from arbitrary detention (Article 9)
▶ the right of persons "deprived of their liberty" to be treated humanely and with respect for their dignity (Article 10)

▶ freedom of movement, including the right to leave one's own country, and not to be arbitrarily denied return to one's own country (Article 12)
▶ the right to a fair trial (Article 14)
▶ the right not to be forced into marriage (Article 23)
▶ the right to equality before the law (Article 26)

The Human Rights Committee has specifically mentioned the risks posed to women in times of conflict and has informed states that they must report to the Committee on all the measures taken in such circumstances to protect women from rape, abduction and other gender-based forms of violence.[59]

ICCPR in time of armed conflict: the possibility of derogation

In harnessing the power of the ICCPR to combat abuses in armed conflict, the advocate must take note of its Article 4. This provision allows states in certain emergency situations which "threaten... the life of the nation" to derogate from (suspend the provision of) certain rights "to the extent strictly required by the exigencies of the situation." (Paragraph 1) Derogation cannot be done in a discriminatory fashion, including on the basis of sex. The derogation must happen in the most limited way and for the shortest time possible, and the notice of derogation must be communicated to the Secretary-General of the UN. No derogation is permissible from those rights deemed non-derogable, or not suspendable, by Article 4(2). These include the rights to life and to be free from torture and ill-treatment, and from slavery.

The International Court of Justice, the principal judicial organ of the UN, has emphasized that the ICCPR continues to function in time of war:

"[T]he protection of the [ICCPR] does not cease in times of war, except by operation of Article 4 of the Covenant whereby certain provisions may be derogated from in a time of national emergency. Respect for the right to life is not, however, such a provision. In principle, the right not arbitrarily to be deprived of one's life applies also in hostilities."[60]

However, the International Court of Justice also concluded that in armed conflict situations the test of what constitutes arbitrary deprivation of life prohibited by the ICCPR is to be determined under "the law applicable in armed conflict" (i.e. international humanitarian law – see below) rather than being "deduced from the terms of the Covenant itself."[61]

Human rights law must not and cannot simply be jettisoned in time of war. To this effect, the Human Rights

Committee has noted, in its first General Comment on the topic of derogation, that "in times of emergency, the protection of human rights becomes all the more important, particularly those rights from which no derogations can be made."[62] In its most recent comment on the issue, General Comment No. 29, the Committee specifically addressed the issue of derogation in armed conflict, as follows:

"During armed conflict, whether international or non-international, rules of international humanitarian law become applicable and help, in addition to the provisions in article 4 and article 5, paragraph 1, of the Covenant, to prevent the abuse of a State's emergency powers. The Covenant requires that even during an armed conflict measures derogating from the Covenant are allowed only if and to the extent that the situation constitutes a threat to the life of the nation."[63]

The Human Rights Committee also reminded states that they cannot derogate from the Covenant in ways that are inconsistent with their other obligations under international law, including particularly international humanitarian law (see below).[64] It has pointed out that aspects of fair trial rights are guaranteed by international humanitarian law and therefore should not be derogated from.[65] In this General Comment, the Human Rights Committee suggested additional rights which contain elements that cannot be subject to derogation. These include: the right to be treated with humanity and dignity when deprived of liberty (Article 10); the prohibitions on hostage-taking, abductions and unacknowledged detention; elements of minority rights related to the prohibition on genocide (see below); deportation or forcible transfer of populations without a valid international legal basis (Article 12); and the prohibition on propaganda for war or racial, national or religious hatred constituting incitement to discriminate or to violence (Article 20).[66] Other provisions so mentioned include the right to an effective remedy (Article 2(3)) and the right to procedural guarantees with regard to non-derogable rights (such as the right to a fair trial when facing the death penalty).[67]

When the Human Rights Committee addressed the issue of equality of rights between men and women in depth, in General Comment No. 28, it also asserted that: "The equal enjoyment of human rights by women must be protected during a state of emergency (Article 4)."[68] Any states that undertake derogations are therefore to inform the Committee of the impact of such measures on women and must affirmatively "demonstrate that they are non-discriminatory."[69]

ICCPR in time of armed conflict: questions of jurisdiction

To apply the ICCPR to an *international* armed conflict, one must also overcome a seeming jurisdictional hurdle.[70] Article 2(1) of the ICCPR states:

"Each State Party to the present Covenant undertakes to respect and to ensure to **all individuals within its territory and subject to its jurisdiction** the rights recognized in the present Covenant, without distinction of any kind..." (emphasis added)

Manfred Nowak, in his authoritative commentary on the ICCPR, addresses this highlighted language. He notes that an "excessively literal reading would... lead to often absurd results."[71] In his view, the purpose for including the clause "within its territory" was to preclude a state's responsibility for rights violations against its own nationals by foreign sovereigns or other parties. However, according to Manfred Nowak:

"(w)hen States Parties... take actions on foreign territory that violate the right of persons subject to its sovereign authority, it would be contrary to the purpose of the Covenant if they could not be held responsible."[72]

Manfred Nowak cites the jurisprudence of the Human Rights Committee to support his view. He notes that in the *Lopez Burgos* case, the Human Rights Committee agreed to hear communications from individuals who had been kidnapped by Uruguayan agents while in neighboring countries, "reasoning that States Parties are responsible for the actions of their agents on foreign territory."[73] Furthermore, in the *Celiberti* case, the Committee noted that the language of Article 2(1),

"does not imply that the State party concerned cannot be held accountable for violations of rights under the Covenant which its agents commit upon the territory of another State, whether with the acquiescence of the Government of that State or in opposition to it."[74]

The *Celiberti* case also concerned the abduction of Uruguayan nationals from abroad by Uruguayan agents. The Human Rights Committee held the Uruguayan state responsible under the ICCPR. Strikingly, the Committee noted that,

"it would be unconscionable to so interpret the responsibility under article 2 of the Covenant as to permit a State party to perpetrate violations of the Covenant on the territory of another State, which violations it could not perpetrate on its own territory."[75]

More recently, the Human Rights Committee has developed an "effective control" test, an approach mirrored by the Committee on Economic, Social and Cultural Rights. This has been written into the Human Rights Committee's authoritative interpretation of Article 2 in the new General Comment on this article.[76] Here the Committee has opined that a state party:

"must respect and ensure the rights laid down in the Covenant to anyone within the power or effective control of that State Party, even if not situated within the territory of the State Party."[77]

Most importantly, this text goes on to specify that:

"This principle also applies to those within the power or effective control of the forces of a State party acting outside its territory, regardless of the circumstances in which such power or effective control was obtained, such as forces constituting a national contingent of a State party assigned to an international peace keeping or peace-enforcement operation."[78]

International Covenant on Economic, Social and Cultural Rights

The International Covenant on Economic, Social and Cultural Rights (ICESCR) is also at the heart of the international legal framework.[79] The ICESCR guarantees the enjoyment of its substantive rights without discrimination of any kind, including on the basis of sex. (Article 2(2)) Furthermore, Article 3 requires state parties to ensure equal rights of men and women in regard to all ICESCR provisions. Substantive rights secured for women by the ICESCR are often affected by war. These rights include the right to work, to enter into marriage only of free will, to an adequate standard of living, including adequate food, clothing and shelter, to freedom from hunger, to the highest possible standard of health and to education.

Beyond the promise of non-discrimination, the only gender-specific provision in this treaty is Article 10(2) which insists that: "Special protection should be accorded to mothers during a reasonable period before and after childbirth." This mirrors the view of international humanitarian law, reflected below.

Unlike the ICCPR, there are no specific derogation provisions included in this Covenant and thus no reason to think that it may be suspended in time of strife. However, the implementation obligation of the state is more modest here than in the case of the ICCPR, and is at all times to "achieve progressively" the promised substantive rights. In contrast, the non-discrimination provision gives rise to an immediate obligation.

Economic sanctions and human rights

Economic sanctions which often precede or accompany conflict may have a dire impact on women and other "vulnerable" groups. Their rights to health and a decent standard of living, as well as their very right to life, may be taken away by sanctions. The Committee on Economic, Social and Cultural Rights, which oversees implementation of the ICESCR, noted this fact and issued an important General Comment on: "The relationship between economic sanctions and respect for economic, social and cultural rights."[80]

While taking no position on the use of sanctions per se, the Committee stressed that the international community must do everything possible to protect the economic, social and cultural rights of populations affected. It must also take such rights into consideration when fashioning sanctions regimes. In addition, any such impact of sanctions must be monitored continuously and steps must be taken to assist vulnerable groups.

States which are subject to sanctions are still fully responsible for economic, social and cultural rights obligations and must also do all they can to mitigate the impact on "vulnerable groups within the society". They must also "ensure the absence of discrimination in relation to the enjoyment of economic, social and cultural rights." (Paragraph 10) However, as the Committee on Economic, Social and Cultural Rights notes: "the inhabitants of a given country do not forfeit their basic economic, social and cultural rights by virtue of any determination that their leaders have violated norms relating to international peace and security." (Paragraph 16)

Convention against Torture

The Convention against Torture and Other Cruel, Inhuman or Degrading Treatment or Punishment (Convention against Torture) reiterates the absolute ban on torture and requires states to take a number of steps to stop and prevent it.[81] These include prosecuting those alleged to have perpetrated torture wherever they may be found, and training law enforcement personnel and all officials, including those in the military, in the prohibition of torture. States must review interrogation practices,

investigate all torture allegations, protect complainants, and guarantee victims redress, rehabilitation and compensation. No one may be returned to a country where she or he may be subjected to torture. (Article 3)

Crucial language is to be found in Article 2(2):

"No exceptional circumstances whatsoever, whether a state of war or a threat of war, internal political instability or any other public emergency, may be invoked as a justification of torture."

Furthermore, superior orders are no justification of torture. (Article 2(3))

The definition of "torture" in Article 1(1) of the Convention against Torture contains four basic elements:

▶ **intention**: the act (causing pain and suffering) was intentional

▶ **severe pain or suffering**: the act caused the victim *"severe pain or suffering, whether physical or mental"*

▶ **purpose**: the act was performed for a prohibited purpose – including intimidation, punishment, obtaining information or a confession but also, importantly, *"for any reason based on discrimination of any kind"*

▶ **official involvement**: the act was performed by officials, or with official consent or acquiescence

The contemporary understanding of rape and other sexual abuse by or with the consent or acquiescence of the state or by organized armed groups is therefore that such abuse constitutes torture or (in the case of certain forms of sexual abuse) ill-treatment.[82] Furthermore, the Special Rapporteur on violence against women, and other international experts, have argued that in certain circumstances violence against women by private individuals, such as domestic violence, should also be considered a form of torture when it reaches the requisite level of severity and when the state fails to exercise due diligence to prevent and punish it.[83]

International Convention on the Elimination of All Forms of Racial Discrimination

Very often, women attacked in times of conflict are targeted not only because of their gender, but also because of their race, national origin or ethnicity, a practice prohibited by the International Convention on the Elimination of All Forms of Racial Discrimination.[84] If states take the necessary steps to fully implement this Convention's provisions to stamp out racial and ethnic discrimination, they will move a long way towards lowering the probability of such violence. Of particular significance is Article 5 which guarantees to all, without distinction "as to race, colour, or national or ethnic origin", among other rights, the "right to security of person and protection by the State against violence or bodily harm, whether inflicted by government officials or by any individual, group or institution".

Genocide Convention

The Convention on the Prevention and Punishment of the Crime of Genocide (Genocide Convention) was one of the first human rights treaties to be drafted in response to the horrors of the Second World War.[85] It was adopted by the UN General Assembly in 1948 and entered into force in 1951. This Convention is considered to form part of customary international law. It prohibits certain human rights abuses when carried out "with intent to destroy, in whole or in part, a national, ethnical, racial or religious groups, as such". (Article 2) Gender is not listed as a specially protected group under the Genocide Convention. However, women are protected as members of all of the other groups listed.

The underlying abuses explicitly mentioned include killings, causing serious harm to members of the group and deliberately inflicting conditions of life calculated to bring about its destruction. Women may be particularly affected by two of the other prohibited means: imposing measures intended to prevent births within the group and forcibly transferring children of the protected group to another group.[86]

In the jurisprudence of international criminal tribunals, in particular in the *Akayesu* case before the International Criminal Tribunal for Rwanda, rape has been found to constitute a form of genocide in certain circumstances. The Tribunal's opinion explained that:

"[i]n patriarchal societies, where membership of a group is determined by the identity of the father, an example of a measure intended to prevent births within a group is the case where, during rape, a woman ... is deliberately impregnated by a man of another group, with the intent to have her give birth to a child who will consequently not belong to its mother's group."... "rape can (also) be a measure intended to prevent births when the person raped refuses subsequently to procreate, in the same way that members of a group can be led, through threats or trauma, not to procreate."[87]

Under the Genocide Convention, states must criminalize acts of genocide, as well as incitement to genocide, (Article 3) including by public officials (Article 4). Under a novel provision found in Article 8, any party may call upon the relevant organs of the UN to "take such action under the Charter of the United Nations as they consider appropriate for the prevention and suppression of acts of genocide..."

Two

6. Discrimination and violence against women in war

"Peace is inextricably linked with equality between women and men"
Beijing Declaration and Platform for Action[88]

"Even in peacetime, women are often handicapped in that education, health and nutrition are not readily accessible to them. Moreover, they are often victims of violence within their own families and communities or at the hands of the State. When war breaks out, tension mounts, living conditions deteriorate and women become particularly vulnerable, especially if they are pregnant or have small children."
International Committee of the Red Cross, *Women and War: Special Brochure* [89]

The prohibition on discrimination against women is a cornerstone of human rights law and, as noted, is non-derogable. Freedom from discrimination, including on grounds of "sex", is the only human right explicitly provided for in the UN Charter, which binds all member states of the UN.[90] In addition, women's right to equality and freedom from discrimination is provided in the Universal Declaration of Human Rights.[91] (Article 2) It is also found in binding international human rights treaties in addition to CEDAW: the ICCPR (Articles 2, 26); the ICESCR (Articles 2(2), 3); and the CRC (Article 2). According to authoritative commentators, the principle of non-discrimination on the grounds of sex is a norm of customary international law.[92]

All of CEDAW's provisions are important to efforts to counter attacks on women in armed conflict. The contemporary understanding of violence against women in

armed conflict grounds such violence in ongoing, pervasive discrimination against women and their subordination in daily life.[93]

Discrimination against women may constitute:

▶ a violation in itself
▶ a cause of violations in conflict
▶ a factor which compounds violations
▶ an obstacle to adequate remedies for abuses

Wartime violence against women is related to "peacetime" assaults on women. Therefore, success for the continuing struggle against sex discrimination is an essential requirement for effectively curtailing or preventing violence against women in conflict.[94] Any state that is serious about doing this must ratify or accede to CEDAW without reservations, if it has not already done so. It must move to lift any limiting reservations it has made, and fully implement all of the Convention's provisions.

Other related and often overlapping types of discrimination, such as those based on race, ethnicity and religion, are often also important in motivating and perpetuating violence against women in conflict. This implicates other international law and standards, including the International Convention on the Elimination of All Forms of Racial Discrimination, the International Convention on the Protection of the Rights of All Migrant Workers and Members of Their Families (MWC),[95] and the UN Declaration on the Elimination of All Forms of Intolerance and of Discrimination Based on Religion or Belief.[96]

Women's right to life in armed conflict

The right to life is one of the most fundamental human rights, and is enshrined in Article 3 of the Universal Declaration of Human Rights, which reads:

"Everyone has the right to life, liberty and security of person."

According to Article 6(1) of the ICCPR,

"Every human being has the inherent right to life. This right shall be protected by law. No one shall be arbitrarily deprived of his life."

The Human Rights Committee has explained that,

"...States have the supreme duty to prevent wars, acts of genocide and other acts of mass violence causing arbitrary loss of life. Every effort they make to avert the danger of war, especially thermonuclear war, and to strengthen international peace and security would constitute the most important condition and guarantee for the safeguarding of the right to life."[97]

Emphasis has been placed on this right in a long string of other instruments. The right to life is non-derogable and applies fully during armed conflicts, as explained above.

However, the ICCPR provision also sets the parameters of the right to life in the context of armed conflict. It indicates that not every killing in armed conflict is a violation of the right to life. Only "arbitrary" deprivations of life are prohibited. The International Court of Justice has determined that whether such

deprivation is arbitrary or not in times of armed conflict would be determined by international humanitarian law. This approach means, roughly, that during armed conflict, killing women combatants during ordinary fighting, or even civilians (as an unintended result of a legitimate attack on a military target which is not disproportionate) may not necessarily constitute a violation of the right to life, although it may still be of grave concern. However, killing or targeting women in any other circumstances is prohibited absolutely as a serious violation of human rights law.

This subject will be discussed further in the section covering international humanitarian law. For now it should be noted that this lower standard of protection of the right to life under an international humanitarian law framework in time of conflict suggests just how much is at risk in a conflict situation. To the extent possible, human rights groups should advocate progressive approaches to international humanitarian law, interpreting it in light of advances in human rights jurisprudence and thinking.[98] A human rights approach to armed conflict goes beyond simply enumerating violations of international humanitarian law. Human rights law itself should also be used to judge the conduct of conflict wherever possible.[99]

Women's right to freedom from torture and ill-treatment

The prohibition of torture and other cruel, inhuman or degrading treatment or punishment is enshrined in Article 5 of the Universal Declaration of Human Rights:

"No one shall be subjected to torture or to cruel, inhuman or degrading treatment or punishment."

Article 7 of the ICCPR repeats this prohibition word for word, adding:

"In particular, no one shall be subjected without his free consent to medical or scientific experimentation."

In addition, the prohibition on torture and other ill-treatment is provided for in many other international treaties and instruments. This prohibition is absolute. The UN devoted a treaty exclusively to the issue of torture and other ill-treatment, the UN Convention against Torture.

According to the UN Convention against Torture, torture is defined as:

"any act by which severe pain or suffering, whether physical or mental, is intentionally inflicted on a person for such purposes as obtaining from him or a third person information or a confession, punishing him for an act he or a third person has committed or is suspected of having committed, or intimidating or coercing him or a third person, or for any reason based on discrimination of any kind, when such pain or suffering is inflicted by or at the instigation of or with the consent or acquiescence of a public official or other person acting in an official capacity."

Hence, practices amounting to torture consist of several key elements:

1) the intentional infliction
2) of severe suffering
3) for a prohibited purpose[100] and
4) by a state agent or with the tacit acceptance by the state.

The UN Convention against Torture offers no specific definition of cruel, inhuman or degrading treatment or punishment. However, the UN General Assembly has subsequently made clear that "the term 'cruel, inhuman or degrading treatment or punishment' should be interpreted so as to extend the widest possible protection against abuses, whether physical or mental..."[101]

Other forms of ill-treatment are also prohibited absolutely. Article 7 of the ICCPR, which prohibits all acts of ill-treatment, is wholly non-derogable. This means that not only torture of women but also cruel, inhuman and degrading treatment or punishment of women are always violations of human rights. Furthermore, as the UN Convention against Torture makes crystal clear, "No exceptional circumstances whatsoever, *whether a state of war or a threat of war*, internal political instability or any other public emergency, may be invoked as a justification of torture."[102] In situations of armed conflict, torture and other cruel, inhuman or degrading treatment or punishment of women are also always violations of international humanitarian law, whether committed by state actors or non-governmental armed groups, in addition to being, in the relevant circumstances, war crimes or crimes against humanity.

Rape and other forms of sexual violence

The contemporary understanding of rape by or with the consent or acquiescence of the state or by organized armed groups is that such abuse constitutes a form of torture.

Amnesty International has affirmed in the past that:

"Under customary international law, many acts of violence against women committed by parties to a conflict (whether international or internal) constitute torture. These include rape and gang rape, abduction and sexual slavery, forced marriage, forced impregnation and forced maternity, sexual mutilation, indecent assault and many other forms of physical violence." [103]

Other forms of sexual abuse may constitute prohibited ill-treatment.

International human rights treaties have not made specific provisions regarding rape and other forms of sexual violence, with the sole exception of the CRC which, in Article 34, obliges states parties to "undertake to protect the child from all forms of sexual exploitation and sexual abuse." This deficiency has to an extent been redressed in international humanitarian law and international criminal law (see below). At any rate, all forms of sexual violence are absolutely prohibited by human rights law, mainly under the prohibition of torture and other ill-treatment, but also as forms of discrimination against women.[104]

Successive UN Special Rapporteurs on torture have affirmed that rape in detention is a form of torture. The first UN Special Rapporteur on torture, Pieter Kooijmans, insisted that,

"...since it was clear that rape or other forms of sexual assault against women in detention were a particularly ignominious violation of the inherent dignity and right to physical integrity of the human being, they accordingly constituted an act of torture."[105]

International courts and tribunals have firmly established that under international law, rape, as well as other forms of sexual violence causing comparably "severe pain or suffering, whether physical or mental," perpetrated either in times of peace or during armed conflict and involving official perpetration, ordering, instigation, consent or acquiescence clearly constitute acts of torture.[106] It should be noted that the defendant in the *Akayesu* case was convicted neither of raping women himself nor of ordering the rape of women (although he did order one act of sexual violence). He nevertheless was convicted of rape because he was an official in a position of responsibility when acts of rape were carried out by his subordinates; and, although aware of them "he took no measures to prevent these acts or punish the perpetrators of them."[107]

States' responsibility goes further than that, to official "consent or acquiescence" for rape perpetrated by non-state actors. The concept of official "consent or acquiescence" is closely linked to states' obligation to exercise due diligence to prevent, investigate and punish violence against women.[108]

As the prohibition of "cruel, inhuman or degrading treatment or punishment" is equally absolute, all acts of sexual abuse of women with the types of official involvement described above, whether as severe as torture or not,[109] are prohibited in all circumstances, and state responsibility may be invoked for such acts in the same way as for torture.[110]

Trafficking

The prohibition of trafficking is a fast-developing area of law, which largely lies beyond the scope of this report.[111] The issue is, however, relevant to armed conflict since, as the UN Office on Drugs and Crime has recognized:

"[I]n many cases, trafficking patterns are also related to conflict situations as combatants (or even peacekeepers) create a market for the services of victims and the effects of conflict erode the capacity of law enforcement and other authorities to combat the problem."[112]

Due to the covert nature of trafficking and the risks involved, including the involvement of criminal gangs, women who are trafficked are extremely vulnerable to violence.

In November 2000, the UN General Assembly adopted the UN Convention against Transnational Organized Crime. This treaty entered into force on 29 September 2003. Annex II to this Convention is comprised of the Protocol to Prevent, Suppress and Punish Trafficking in Persons, Especially Women and Children,[113] which entered into force on 25 December 2003. One of this Protocol's innovative provisions is that it is open not only to ratification by all states that have ratified the underlying Convention, but also to regional economic integration organizations (such as the European Union) when at least one state member of such an entity is also a party to the Protocol. (Article 16)

Some commentators working on a practical level with victims of trafficking perceive this Protocol as a law enforcement instrument, rather than one geared towards human rights.[114] This is significant because advocates warn that a strictly criminal justice approach to the issue may endanger trafficked persons, leading to their deportation or imprisonment, or forcing them underground or leading to

their being re-trafficked.[115] However, the Protocol purports to see its mission as to "protect the victims of... trafficking, including by protecting their internationally recognized human rights". (Preamble) One of its main purposes is "to prevent and combat trafficking in persons, paying particular attention to women and children". (Article 2(a))

The Protocol defines "trafficking" in Article 3(a) as follows:

"the recruitment, transportation, transfer, harbouring or receipt of persons, by means of the threat or use of force or other forms of coercion, of abduction, of fraud, of deception, of the abuse of power or of a position of vulnerability or of the giving or receiving of payments or benefits to achieve the consent[116] of a person having control over another person, for the purpose of exploitation."[117]

All states are to criminalize such practices in full, including establishing offences for those who are accomplices and those who direct and organize such offences. (Article 5) States must offer full assistance and protection to the victims of trafficking, as well as means of obtaining compensation (Article 6). This could include: counselling, medical assistance, and educational programmes designed to take into account the gender of the victims. (Article 6(3) and 6(4))

States are also to consider, on humanitarian grounds, allowing victims of trafficking to remain in their territory on either a temporary or permanent basis, in appropriate cases. (Article 7) Home states are to facilitate the safe return of such individuals. (Article 8) All states are to strengthen border controls so as to assist in the detection and prevention of trafficking, but "(w)ithout prejudice to international commitments in relation to the free movement of people". (Article 11(1))

States have to take full measures to prevent trafficking, including through cooperation with non-governmental organizations (Article 9) and international information exchange and training for law enforcement and other relevant personnel. (Article 10) The training should incorporate consideration of "gender-sensitive issues". (Article 10(3)).

A crucial "saving clause" is included in Article 14. This stipulates that the Protocol's implementation is not to affect "the rights, obligations and responsibilities of States and individuals under international law, including international humanitarian law and international human rights law" as well as international refugee law. (Article

14(1)) Furthermore, the Protocol is not to be interpreted in a manner which discriminates against victims of trafficking, and is to be implemented in a manner fully consistent with international human rights guarantees of non-discrimination. (Article 14)

The Principles and Guidelines on Human Rights and Trafficking of the UN High Commissioner for Human Rights, and general international law relating to refugees, provide further protection to persons trafficked during armed conflicts.[118]

Although trafficked women and girls are often penalized under domestic immigration laws, Amnesty International holds that they should be treated as victims of human rights abuse. Often their rights have been violated by state actors, such as border guards demanding sexual services to let them pass. Given draconian immigration controls, trafficking may be the only way they can escape persecution and war in their own countries. Criminal sanctions should focus on traffickers, whereas the victims of trafficking should be treated in the same way as any other victim of gender-based violence.

Sexual slavery

Systematic rape, sexual slavery and slavery-like practices during armed conflict continue to be widespread, as has been recently reiterated by the UN High Commissioner for Human Rights.[119] These practices clearly constitute the most serious violations of human rights norms, international humanitarian law and international criminal law.

Reports of sexual slavery during war at the hands of various parties to the conflict have been received from many countries, including Afghanistan, Burundi, Colombia, the Democratic Republic of the Congo, Liberia, Myanmar and Sierra Leone, according to the Special Rapporteur of the Sub-Commission on the Promotion and Protection of Human Rights on systematic rape, sexual slavery and slavery-like practices, Gay McDougall.[120] The archetypal example of this practice remains the system employed by the Japanese Imperial Army during the Second World War, when the so-called "comfort women" from countries across Asia were forced into military sexual slavery. Systematic rape was a part of the Rwandan genocide during which, according to the High Commissioner for Human Rights, between 250,000 and 500,000 women were raped. Survivors of these atrocities have worked hard to bring such horrors to light, and continue to campaign for justice and adequate reparation.

The Special Rapporteur of the Sub-Commission on the Promotion and Protection of Human Rights on systematic rape, sexual slavery and slavery-like practices has defined sexual slavery as, "the status or condition of a person over whom any or all of the powers attaching to the right of ownership are exercised, including sexual access through rape or other forms of sexual abuse."[121] As she has written in simpler form, "Slavery, when combined with sexual violence, constitutes sexual slavery."[122]

Given that sexual slavery is a form of slavery, its prohibition rises to the level of a *jus cogens* norm, the highest kind of international norm, and is prohibited at all times and in all places.[123] Universal jurisdiction applies to such a crime and it can be prosecuted by any state. In fact, all states have an obligation to bring the alleged perpetrators of such heinous crimes to justice, wherever the offence occurred. Holding perpetrators accountable is a crucial deterrent to sexual slavery and similar abuses. As the Commission on Human Rights has asserted, the expectation of impunity encourages such violence to continue unabated.[124]

The Rome Statute of the International Criminal Court explicitly includes sexual slavery as a constituent act of crimes against humanity when part of a widespread or systematic attack directed against a civilian population. Furthermore, sexual slavery is designated a war crime in international armed conflict (Article 8(2)(b)(xxii)) and in internal armed conflict (Article 8(2)(e)(vi)). The new International Criminal Court should be strongly encouraged to vigorously investigate and prosecute such offences.

The Sub-Commission on the Promotion and Protection of Human Rights has interpreted the Rome Statute of the International Criminal Court as including sexual slavery as a possible constituent act of genocide in certain circumstances, following on from the important jurisprudence of the *ad hoc* tribunals for the Former Yugoslavia and Rwanda.[125] In the newer Special Court for Sierra Leone, defendants have been charged in connection with cases of sexual slavery, according to the High Commissioner for Human Rights.[126] Innovatively, the Sierra Leone Special Court can also prosecute "forced marriage," a similar practice in many conflicts, as a form of sexual violence.

However, international prosecutions alone cannot adequately stamp out sexual slavery and related practices. They must be accompanied by effective action throughout the international community and at the national level. The Special Rapporteur has made the following recommendations to states as to how to combat sexual slavery and related practices. States should:[127]

▶ enact special legislation incorporating international human rights, humanitarian and criminal law into their national legal systems which provides for universal jurisdiction over the crime of sexual slavery

▶ search for people alleged to have committed such offences and bring them to justice

▶ make sure that prosecutors address sexual slavery from a gender-sensitive perspective; for example, according to the Special Rapporteur, the defence of consent should not be allowed when the sexual assault is charged and prosecuted as slavery[128]

▶ provide training for military and security forces which explicitly addresses the prohibition of sexual slavery

▶ make sure that appropriate disciplinary mechanisms are put into place and used in addition to appropriate criminal penalties

▶ provide adequate protection for victims and witnesses and appropriate services for victims, especially reproductive and gynaecological healthcare services

▶ make sure that peace agreements contain provisions to ensure effective investigation and redress of sexual slavery; and following such agreements the authorities must prepare to deal with the possible escalation of such violence against women in the post-conflict era

Preventive action must be taken against sexual slavery, since by the time reports surface, it is too late for many victims. To this end, the Sub-Commission on the Promotion and Protection of Human Rights for its part has encouraged states to promote human rights education on systematic rape, sexual slavery and slavery-like practices.[129] The Sub-Commission expressed the view that this could both prevent future violations and ensure the accuracy of historical accounts.

Forced pregnancy

A related atrocity is the practice of forced pregnancy. This has been defined in the Rome Statute of the International Criminal Court statute as the "unlawful confinement of a woman forcibly made pregnant with the intent of affecting the ethnic composition of any population or carrying out other grave violations of international law". (Article 7(2)(f)). Simply stated, this involves the detention of women made pregnant through rape until abortion is no longer a feasible option.[130] Forced pregnancy was frequently reported in the war in Bosnia-Herzegovina, according to the 1992 Final Report of the Commission of Experts Established Pursuant to Security Council Resolution 780.[131]

Under the Rome Statute of the International Criminal Court , forced pregnancy may be a war crime in either international (Article 8(2)(b)(xxii)) or internal armed conflict (Article 8(2)(e)(vi)). It may also constitute a crime against humanity when part of a widespread or systematic attack against a civilian population either in time of conflict or not (Article 7(1)(g). As the Women's Initiatives for Gender Justice has underscored, it "is a violent crime, committed with a violent intent, and it causes extreme suffering for the victim."[132]

Two

Amnesty International

7. Regional standards affecting women

Two

Many excellent regional treaties and non-treaty standards govern human rights. Here only those with particular emphasis on violence against women are reviewed.

Regional treaties

Inter-American Convention on the Prevention, Punishment and Eradication of Violence Against Women

The Organization of American States (OAS) adopted the Inter-American Convention on the Prevention, Punishment and Eradication of Violence Against Women[133] in 1994 and it entered into force in 1995, the same year as the UN Fourth World Conference on Women in Beijing. It is the first international treaty which specifically deals with the subject of violence against women. Thus, it is a hard law source, but is only applicable to those member states of the OAS who choose to ratify it. (Article 17 allows "any other state" to choose to accede to the Convention through the OAS.) According to the Inter-American Commission of Women, the Convention has 31 state parties to date.[134] OAS member states which have not ratified the Convention, and should be encouraged to do so, include Canada, Jamaica and the USA.

The scope of this Convention is broad, defining violence against women as "any act or conduct, based on gender, which causes death or physical, sexual or psychological harm or suffering to women, whether in the public or private sphere." (Article 1) It takes a strong rights-based approach to the issue, similar to CEDAW

Committee General Recommendation 19, proclaiming that "every woman has the right to be free from violence in both the public and private spheres" (Article 3) and listing the constituent rights which make up this compound right (Articles 4, 5 and 6).

The Convention does not include any provisions that explicitly address the situation of women in conflict. However, a number of its general provisions are relevant.

States agree to:

▶ "prevent, punish and eradicate" violence against women (Article 7)
▶ refrain from acts of violence against women (Article 7a)
▶ apply "due diligence" to prevent and redress violence against women (Article 7b)
▶ adopt the legislation necessary to effectively ensure these measures and to protect victims (Article 7c, d, e, f, g)

They also agree progressively to:

▶ promote awareness of women's rights to be free from violence (Article 8a)
▶ modify underlying social and cultural patterns regarding gender (Article 8b)
▶ promote gender training of law enforcement personnel (Article 8c)
▶ offer shelters and counselling to victims (Article 8d)

All measures taken to fulfil these treaty obligations are to be reported to the Inter-American Commission of Women. (Article 10) Either the Commission or any state party to the Convention may request advisory opinions from the Inter-American Court of Human Rights on

28

the interpretation of this Convention. (Article 11) Furthermore, individuals or non-governmental organizations may bring complaints of violations of Article 7 of the Convention by a state party to the Inter-American Commission on Human Rights.

The African Union Protocol on the Rights of Women in Africa

The African Union Protocol on the Rights of Women in Africa, adopted and opened for signature by the African Union in July 2003, requires governments to eliminate violence against women, as well as gender discrimination.[135] It will enter into force following ratification by the required number of 15 states.[136] Its implementation will be monitored by the African Commission on Human and Peoples' Rights.

Innovatively, the Protocol defines "violence against women" as:

"all acts perpetrated against women which cause or could cause them physical, sexual, psychological, and economic harm, including the threat to take such acts; or to undertake the imposition of arbitrary restrictions on or deprivation of fundamental freedoms in private or public life in peace time and during situations of armed conflicts or of war" (Article 1(j))

The Protocol requires governments to take the following steps to combat violence against women (Article 4):

▶ enact and enforce the needed laws
▶ adopt the necessary legislative, administrative and other measures to prevent, punish and eradicate violence against women
▶ engage in anti-discrimination education
▶ punish the perpetrators
▶ assist with the rehabilitation of victims
▶ provide adequate resources for the activities listed
▶ ensure that women have equal access to refugee determination procedures and that women are accorded the full protection of international refugee law
▶ not carry out the death penalty on pregnant or nursing women

The Protocol guarantees to women the right to dignity and respect for her person (Article 3); the right to life and freedom from exploitation and cruel, inhuman or degrading treatment or punishment (Article 4); the right to equality in marriage and divorce (Article 7); and to be married only by free consent (Article 6); access to justice and equal protection before the law (Article 8); the right to adequate food and drinking water (Article 15); and the right to participation in governance and decision-making (Article 9). They shall also have the right to equal access to education (Article 12) and other economic, social and cultural rights (Article 13).

Women's reproductive rights and health receive particular attention in Article 14, including the right to control their fertility and to choose the number and spacing of their children, the right to contraception and the right to be protected against "sexually transmitted infections", including HIV/AIDS. For the first time in international law, the Protocol guarantees the right to abortion in case of sexual assault, rape, incest and when the pregnancy endangers the mental or physical health of the mother (Article 14(2)(c)).[137] Governments must also prohibit and condemn "harmful practices" such as female genital mutilation. A unique provision guarantees the rights of widows, including the right to be free from inhuman, humiliating or degrading treatment, to automatically become the guardian of her children after the death of her husband, to have an equitable share in the inheritance (Article 21) and the right to remarry (Article 20). Women are provided with broad rights to a positive cultural context, to a healthy and sustainable environment and to sustainable development. States shall provide remedies for violations of all these rights. (Article 25)

Given Africa's recent conflicts and their tragic impact on women, Article 11 pertinently provides specific guarantees for women in such situations:

▶ states must respect and ensure respect for international humanitarian law, paying particular attention to its protections for women (Article 11(1)) and must protect women civilians in conflict (11(2))
▶ states are to protect women asylum-seekers, refugees, returnees and internally displaced persons from all violence, rape and other sexual exploitation (11(3))
▶ states must consider acts of rape and sexual violence in conflict as war crimes, genocide and/or crimes against humanity (11(3))
▶ states must see that perpetrators of such crimes are brought to justice (11(3))
▶ states must make sure that no girls under 18 years old take a direct part in hostilities (11(4))
▶ states must make sure that children are not recruited as soldiers (11(4))

Underlying these guarantees is women's basic right to peace, set out in Article 10. This includes their right to increased participation in conflict prevention, decision-making, protection of refugees and the internally displaced, and all aspects of post-conflict reconstruction and rehabilitation. In keeping with the right to peace, states are directed to reduce their military expenditures "significantly" and to use the funds instead for social development, especially with regards to women. (Article 10(3)) Given its innovative and relevant provisions, all African countries should be strongly urged to ratify this instrument as soon as possible so that it will enter into force.

Other regional standards

Council of Europe: Recommendation Rec(2002)5 of the Committee of Ministers to Member States on the protection of women against violence

The Council of Europe's Recommendation Rec(2002)5 of the Committee of Ministers to member states on the protection of women against violence sets out a range of measures that should be taken to stamp out violence against women. The foundation of this non-treaty standard is the state obligation to use "due diligence" (Paragraph II) to prevent, investigate and punish both private and state violence against women.

The requisite tasks also include:

▶ reviewing legislation and policies with respect to violence against women, so as to ensure that women actually are guaranteed their rights, and non-governmental organizations are involved in the elaboration and implementation of necessary measures (Paragraph I 1,2,3)

▶ encouraging the active participation of men in action to end violence against women (Paragraph III)

▶ drawing up plans of action, and promoting research and study on the topic (Paragraphs IV, V, VI)

▶ improving coordination in efforts to combat violence (Paragraphs I(3), VII)

▶ reporting to the Council of Europe on follow up measures taken (Paragraph IX)

An Appendix attached to Recommendation Rec (2002)5 sets out more detailed actions to be taken. It also notes expressly that for the purposes of this standard, violence against women includes "violation of the human rights of women in situations of armed conflict, in particular the taking of hostages, forced displacement, systematic rape, sexual slavery, forced pregnancy, and trafficking for the purposes of sexual exploitation and economic exploitation". (Appendix, Paragraph 1d)

In the Appendix, the Council of Europe Committee of Ministers calls on member states to take a number of steps to deal with violence against women, in general. Many of these mirror standards at the international level. Measures to be taken include:

▶ increasing public awareness and training programmes, especially for law enforcement and the judiciary, with regard to violence against women (Appendix, para. 3(d), 3(e), 7, 8, 11, 13)

▶ combating gender stereotypes in education and the media (Appendix, para. 15, 17-20)

▶ offering treatment and counselling for victims and preventing re-victimization through gender-insensitive enforcement polices and personnel (Appendix, paras. 23-33)

▶ criminalization of all forms of rape and sexual assault (Appendix, paras. 34-35)

▶ providing for compensation for victims (Appendix, para. 36)

Some innovative provisions are explicitly enumerated in this standard. They tell states to, among other things:

▶ consider the needs of preventing gender-based violence while engaging in local, regional and urban planning and planning services such as transportation and public lighting and the design of buildings (Appendix, para. 21-22)

▶ provide that victims of violence have the opportunity to be heard by female officers (Appendix, para. 29)

▶ penalize any sexual act committed against a non-consenting person, regardless of whether that person displays signs of resistance or not (Appendix, para. 35)

▶ organize intervention programmes for perpetrators (Appendix, paras. 50-53)

▶ consider setting up genetic data banks with genetic profiles of perpetrators of sexual violence (Appendix, para. 54)

Additional measures concerning violence in conflict and post-conflict situations

Specific measures that should be taken to protect women from violence in conflict and post-conflict zones are set out in detail in the Appendix. The measures recommended by the Council of Europe Recommendation include the following:

Member states should:

"68. penalise all forms of violence against women and children in situations of conflict, in accordance with the provisions of international humanitarian law, whether they occur in the form of humiliation, torture, sexual slavery or death resulting from these actions;

"69. penalise rape, sexual slavery, forced pregnancy, enforced sterilisation or any other form of sexual violence of comparable gravity as an intolerable violation of human rights, as crimes against humanity and, when committed in the context of an armed conflict, as war crimes;

"70. ensure protection of witnesses before the national courts and international criminal tribunals trying genocide, crimes against humanity and war crimes, and provide them with legal residence at least during the proceedings;

"71. ensure social and legal assistance to all persons called to testify before the national courts and international criminal tribunals trying genocide, crimes against humanity and war crimes;

"72. consider providing refugee status or subsidiary protection for reasons of gender-based persecution and/or providing residence status on humanitarian grounds to women victims of violence during conflicts;

"73. support and fund NGOs providing counselling and assistance to victims of violence during conflicts and in post-conflict situations;

"74. in post-conflict situations, promote the inclusion of issues specific to women into the reconstruction and the political renewal process in affected areas;

"75. at national and international levels, ensure that all interventions in areas which have been affected by conflicts are performed by personnel who have been offered gender-sensitive training;

"76. support and fund programmes which follow a gender-sensitive approach in providing assistance to victims of conflicts and contributing to the reconstruction and repatriation efforts following a conflict."

Two

8. Universal non-treaty standards specific to women

A number of significant non-treaty standards have been developed to further specify what states and others must do to protect women and girls in armed conflict. Unlike treaties, or rules that clearly rise to the level of customary international law, these standards do not as such constitute binding legal obligations on states. They do, however, provide detail and clarification of existing legal rules, as well as prospects for their future development. With increasing repetition of many of these provisions and their consistent acceptance by states in the form, *inter alia*, of UN General Assembly resolutions, there is an increasingly powerful argument available that at least parts of some of these texts are emerging norms of customary international law.

Declaration on the Protection of Women and Children in Emergency and Armed Conflict

Born out of the work of the UN Commission on the Status of Women at sessions in 1972 and 1974, the Declaration on the Protection of Women and Children in Emergency and Armed Conflict was adopted by the UN General Assembly in December 1974.[138] The aim of the declaration is to "provide special protection of women and children belonging to the civilian population" (preamble) and its own terms "call... for the strict observance of the Declaration by all Member States (of the UN)." (Preamble)

Although it does not make specific reference to rape, sexual assault or other gender-based violence, the

Declaration is significant because it represents the first real recognition within the UN system of the need to address the specific threats to women in armed conflict. Also, its text and drafting process influenced the Additional Protocols to the Geneva Conventions (see below) which were being drafted in the 1970s.[139]

The Declaration on the Protection of Women and Children in Emergency and Armed Conflict:

▶ prohibits attacks and bombings on the civilian population (Paragraph 1)
▶ "severely" condemns the use of chemical and bacteriological weapons (Paragraph 2)
▶ calls on states to respect the Geneva Conventions and other international law to protect women and children (Paragraph 3)
▶ deems "criminal" all forms of repression, cruel and inhuman treatment, imprisonment, torture, shooting, mass arrests, collective punishment, destruction of dwellings and forcible eviction of women and children (Paragraph 5)

Significantly, civilian women and children caught in situations of emergency and conflict are not to be deprived of "shelter, food, medical aid or other inalienable rights, in accordance with the Universal Declaration of Human Rights, the International Covenant on Civil and Political Rights, the International Covenant on Economic, Social and Cultural Rights, the Declaration on the Rights of the Child or other instruments of international law". (Paragraph 6)

Declaration on the Elimination of Violence against Women

Unfortunately, after the adoption of the 1974 UN General Assembly Declaration on the Protection of Women and Children in Emergency and Armed Conflict, little attention was given to the issue of women in conflict until the early 1990s. In response to the widely publicized gender-based atrocities in the armed conflict in the former Yugoslavia, and the courageous revelations of the aging former "comfort women" forced into sexual slavery during the Second World War, the international women's human rights movement galvanized the international community to take notice of the issue. Hence, during the 1990s, a corpus of international standards crystallized which focused on state obligations to protect women from gender-based violence, including in war. Many of the most relevant standards date from this era.

One of the most important of these is the 1993 UN General Assembly Declaration on the Elimination of Violence against Women.[140] This Declaration constituted affirmation by the international community of a number of important realities, including:

▶ "violence against women is an obstacle to the achievement of equality, development and peace" (Preamble)
▶ "violence against women constitutes a violation of the rights and fundamental freedoms of women" (Preamble)
▶ "violence against women is a manifestation of historically unequal power relations between men and women, which have led to domination over and discrimination against women by men and to the prevention of the full advancement of women, and that violence against women is one of the crucial social mechanisms by which women are forced into a subordinate position compared with men..." (Preamble)

These constitute an important and authoritative recognition of the holistic view of violence against women, as both a cause and consequence of women's subordination in society, and inherently linked to pervasive discrimination against women. Furthermore, violence against women is a fundamental human rights issue, not a private matter. It is within this serious context, and not as an aberration, that violence against women in armed conflict should be understood.

All forms of gender-based violence against women in armed conflict are clearly included within the scope of the Declaration which specifies its relevance to "violence occurring in the family" (Article 2a), "violence occurring within the general community" (Article 2b) and "violence perpetrated or condoned by the State, wherever it occurs" (Article 2c). Furthermore, the preamble specifically registers concern that "some groups of women, such as... refugee women... and women in situations of armed conflict, are especially vulnerable to violence".

Once the Declaration. enumerates these basic concerns and frameworks, it sets out the requirements on states. These state obligations are concentrated in Article 4.

States should:

▶ condemn violence against women (Article 4)
▶ not invoke any custom, tradition or religious consideration to avoid their obligations to this end (Article 4)
▶ consider ratifying CEDAW or withdrawing any reservations they have entered to that Convention (Article 4a)
▶ refrain from engaging in violence against women (Article 4b)
▶ exercise due diligence to prevent, investigate and punish acts of violence against women, by state or private actors (Article 4c)
▶ develop legal and administrative sanctions in domestic law for perpetrators of violence against women (Article 4d)
▶ develop legal avenues of redress for women victim-survivors of violence (Article 4d)
▶ make sure that the sanctions and redress available are actually accessible to women and that women are informed of their rights (Article 4d)
▶ ensure gender-sensitive enforcement of sanctions and redress for women victim-survivors (Article 4f)
▶ cooperate with non-governmental organizations (Article 4e, 4o, 4p)
▶ commit sufficient budgetary resources for these activities (Article 4h)
▶ develop preventive approaches and not simply punish after the fact (Article 4f)
▶ offer rehabilitation, treatment, support and assistance to women victim-survivors (Article 4g)
▶ tackle stereotypical views of women and men through education (Article 4j)
▶ promote the study of violence against women with a view to understanding and stopping it (Article 4k)
▶ encourage inter-governmental organizations to combat violence against women (Article 4q)

It must be noted that the Declaration on the Elimination of Violence against Women is not a convention or treaty. It is not a primary source of inter-national law. However, UN General Assembly resolutions are authoritative statements of the international com-munity. For example, the touchstone of the International Bill of Human Rights, the Universal Declaration of Human Rights, is also a UN General Assembly resolution.

Such resolutions may be understood as either evidence of a primary source of international law, or movement in the direction of new norms of international law. A number of factors are considered in evaluating any given resolution as evidence of a customary norm or as a developing norm. These include the kind of language used, which is often hortatory, providing encouragement rather than imposing obligations. For example, Article 4 says that states "should" undertake the enumerated actions. Other factors include the repetition of such resolutions and voting patterns.

There are several other arguments which can also be made.

The preamble of the Declaration notes that respect for this resolution would strengthen efforts at "effective implementation" of CEDAW, which is a treaty or primary source of international law. As such, the Declaration may be seen as a kind of codicil to CEDAW and states parties would need to take it into consideration in order to fully respect their treaty obligations.

The Declaration understands itself as "a clear and comprehensive definition of violence against women, a clear statement of the rights to be applied to ensure the elimination of violence against women in all its forms, a commitment by States in respect of their responsibilities, and a commitment by the international community at large to the elimination of violence against women". (Preamble) Furthermore, the UN General Assembly "urges that every effort be made so that it becomes generally... respected". In sum, the Declaration represents one of the most specific statements made to date by the international community, at a high political level, of what states must do to end violence against women.

Beijing Declaration and Platform for Action

The Beijing Declaration and Platform for Action, which came out of the 1995 UN Fourth World Conference on Women, has two sections which are particularly relevant to the prevention of violence against women in armed conflict.[141]

Beijing Platform for Action: Violence against Women

As in the UN General Assembly Declaration on the Elimination of Violence against Women, violence against women is recognized in the Beijing Platform for Action as "an obstacle to... equality, development and peace". (Paragraph 112) This section of the Beijing Platform for Action makes specific reference to "violation of the human rights of women in situations of armed conflict, in particular murder, systematic rape, sexual slavery and forced pregnancy" (Paragraph 114) as forms of violence against women covered by its provisions. It also notes the particular vulnerability of women to violence in such situations, including "armed conflict, foreign occupation, wars of aggression, civil wars, terrorism, including hostage-taking". (Paragraph 116)

The holistic approach to violence against women seen in the Declaration on the Elimination of Violence against Women is carried through here, explicitly linking violence to discrimination and women's subordination. (Paragraphs 117, 118)

In thinking about the role of law in the process of combating violence against women in armed conflict, it is instructive to note that according to the Beijing Platform for Action, violence against women is worsened by, among other factors:

"women's lack of access to legal information, aid or protection; the lack of laws that effectively prohibit violence against women; failure to reform existing laws; inadequate efforts on the part of public authorities to promote awareness of and enforce existing laws."(Paragraph 118)

On the issue of violence against women in conflict, this section of the Beijing Platform for Action insists that the training of all officials in humanitarian law and human rights law and the punishment of perpetrators would lessen the likelihood of such violence. (Paragraph 121) It further requires that governments "and other actors" should mainstream gender perspectives in all policies and programmes, "so that before decisions are taken an analysis may be made of their effects on women and men". (Paragraph 123)

A series of strategic objectives is identified relating to each of the 12 principal areas of concern recognized by the Beijing Platform for Action. Each strategic objective is complemented by lists of tasks which states are asked to undertake in order to meet that goal. The most relevant strategic objectives relating to violence against women in conflict are that states should: "take integrated measures to prevent and eliminate violence against women" (Strategic objective D.1); "Study the causes and consequences of violence against women and the effectiveness of preventive measures" (Strategic objective D.2); and "Eliminate trafficking in women and assist victims of violence due to prostitution and trafficking" (Strategic objective D.3).

Integrated measures to prevent and eliminate violence against women

In order to successfully "take integrated measures to prevent and eliminate violence against women (Strategic objective D.1), states must, among other things:

▶ condemn violence and not use cultural justifications for it (Paragraph 124a)
▶ refrain from violence against women (Paragraph 124b)
▶ exercise due diligence to prevent, investigate and punish violence against women by private or public actors (Paragraph 124b)
▶ enact or strengthen legal and administrative sanctions for all forms of violence against women and ensure that they are accessible to the women who need them (Paragraph 124c, i)
▶ periodically review such legislation (Paragraph 124d)
▶ take measures to ensure compensation of victims (Paragraph 124d)
▶ ratify and implement relevant international human rights treaties (Paragraph 124e)
▶ implement CEDAW, taking into account General Recommendation 19 (Paragraph 124f)
▶ give gender-sensitive training, especially to judicial, legal, law enforcement and medical personnel and those who work with refugees and migrants (Paragraph 124gn)
▶ inform women of rights and remedies available to them (Paragraph 124h)
▶ "ensure that the revictimization of women victims of violence does not occur because of gender-insensitive laws or judicial or enforcement practices" (Paragraph 124g)
▶ support non-governmental organizations in their efforts to combat harmful traditional practices that constitute violence against women (Paragraph 124i)
▶ adopt plans of action to end violence against women (Paragraph 124j)
▶ combat stereotypical views of gender roles, including through education (Paragraph 124k)
▶ create or strengthen complaints procedures that are victim-friendly (Paragraph 124l)
▶ provide for the particular needs of women with disabilities (Paragraph 124m)
▶ allocate adequate resources to all these ends (Paragraph 124p)

▶ include relevant information in all submissions to UN human rights bodies (Paragraph 124q)
▶ cooperate with and assist all relevant human rights mechanisms, such as the UN Special Rapporteurs on violence against women and on torture (Paragraph 124r)

Governments, including local governments, and other relevant actors must also:

▶ provide shelters, medical and counselling services and appropriate assistance to victims (Paragraph 125a),
▶ make sure that services are accessible to and effective for migrant women and girls (Paragraph 125b,c)
▶ organize community-based education and training and information campaigns (Paragraph 125e,g)
▶ develop programmes to eliminate sexual harassment (Paragraph 126a)
▶ carry out education about how acts of violence against women constitute crimes and human rights violations (Paragraph 126b)
▶ take special measures to protect women at risk of violence, including specifically refugee and internally displaced women (Paragraph 126d)

Study the causes and consequences of violence against women

In order to fulfil the objective "Study the causes and consequences of violence against women and the effectiveness of preventive measures" (Strategic objective D.2) , states must:

▶ promote research, collect data and compile statistics on violence against women, especially that which can assist in prevention or documents the impact of violence (Paragraph 129a, c)
▶ publicize the findings of such research (Paragraph 129b)
▶ encourage consideration of these issues by the media (Paragraph 129d)

Eliminate trafficking in women

To achieve the objective "Eliminate trafficking in women and assist victims of violence due to prostitution and trafficking"(Strategic objective D.3), states must

▶ ratify and enforce relevant treaties (Paragraph 130a)
▶ address root causes (Paragraph 130b)
▶ promote cooperation among law enforcement agencies and services (Paragraph 130c)
▶ offer rehabilitation, job training, legal assistance and so on to victims of trafficking (Paragraph 130d)
▶ cooperate with non-governmental organizations working in the field (Paragraph 130d)

▶ develop education programmes and legislation to prevent sex tourism and trafficking in children (Paragraph 130e)

Beijing Platform for Action: women and armed conflict

Perhaps most importantly, this section of the Beijing Platform for Action proclaims that, "Peace is inextricably linked with equality between women and men and development". (Paragraph 131) It condemns gross abuses of human rights in armed conflict, including rape and systematic rape, and tells states that perpetrators must be brought to justice.(Paragraph 131) Furthermore, the Beijing Platform for Action insists on the mainstreaming of gender perspectives into all policies and programmes related to armed conflict. (Paragraph 141)

Experts have pointed out that one of the important contributions of the Beijing Platform for Action is the articulation of a broad view of women in armed conflict, including, but not limited to, as victims of sexual violence. The Beijing Platform for Action looks at a wide range of issues that have an impact on women in conflict and this broader view has been taken up in subsequent work on the topic at the international level. Furthermore, the mere fact that this topic was chosen as one of only 12 areas of principal concern in the Beijing Platform for Action has flagged its importance to the international community.[142]

The Beijing Platform for Action lists several strategic objectives in relation to violence against women in armed conflict and sets out recommendations for actions to be taken to meet each objective.

Increase the participation of women in conflict resolution and protect women

"Increase the participation of women in conflict resolution at decision-making levels and protect women living in situations of armed and other conflicts or under foreign occupation" (Strategic Objective E.1)

Actions to be taken to meet this objective include:

▶ promoting equal participation of women in decision-making, including at the UN (Paragraph 142a)
▶ aiming for gender balance on international criminal tribunals, judicial bodies and those related to peaceful resolution of disputes (Paragraph 142b)
▶ providing gender issues training to all those involved in such bodies (Paragraph 142c)

Reduce excessive military expenditures and control arms

"Reduce excessive military expenditures and control the availability of armaments" (Strategic Objective E.2)

Governments must:

▶ increase conversion of military resources to peaceful ends (Paragraph 143a)
▶ move resources from military spending to social spending for the advancement of women (Paragraph 143b)
▶ combat illicit arms trafficking (Paragraph 143d)
▶ combat trafficking in women (Paragraph 143d)
▶ recognize that women (and children) are disproportionately harmed by the use of landmines (Paragraph 143e)
▶ promote mine clearance (Paragraph 143(e)(iii))
▶ adopt moratoria on export of anti-personnel landmines (Paragraph 143e (v))
▶ recognize the leading role that women have played in the peace movement (Paragraph 143f)
▶ work actively towards general, complete and verifiable disarmament (Paragraph 143f (i))

Reduce the incidence of human rights abuse in conflicts

"Promote non-violent forms of conflict resolution and reduce the incidence of human rights abuse in conflict situations" (Strategic objective E.3)

The list of measures to be taken includes:

▶ ratifying treaties concerning protection of women in conflict, including the Fourth Geneva Convention of 1949 and both the 1977 Additional Protocols (Paragraph 144a)
▶ respecting in totality the norms of international humanitarian law (see below), especially those to protect women from rape, forced prostitution and other forms of "indecent assault" (Paragraph 144b)
▶ encouraging peaceful resolution of disputes (Paragraph 145b)
▶ condemning the use of systematic rape and torture of women as a tool of war (Paragraph 145c)
▶ providing victims of systematic rape and ill-treatment of women in conflict with full assistance for physical and mental rehabilitation (Paragraph 145c)
▶ reaffirming that rape in war constitutes a war crime and that it may also, in certain circumstances, be a crime against humanity or an act of genocide (145d)
▶ taking all needed measures to protect women from rape, and strengthening mechanisms to investigate allegations of rape and bring perpetrators to justice (Paragraph 145d)

- upholding and reinforcing the standards of international humanitarian law and human rights law to prevent all violence against women in conflict (Paragraph 145e)
- investigating fully all acts of violence against women during conflict, including forced prostitution and sexual slavery (Paragraph 145e)
- prosecuting all those implicated in war crimes against women (Paragraph 145e)
- providing full redress to women victims (Paragraph 145e)
- incorporating gender into training for all relevant personnel, especially those who are to participate in peace-keeping and aid operations (Paragraph 145g)
- refraining absolutely from using food and medicine as tools for political pressure (Paragraph 145h)
- taking steps to alleviate the impact of sanctions on women (Paragraph 145i)

Promote women's contribution to peace
"Promote women's contribution to fostering a culture of peace" (Strategic objective E.4)

Relevant required steps include:

- promotion of peace education and research (Paragraphs 146)
- encouraging research on the impact of conflict on women, and involving women in the research (Paragraph 146b)

Protect and support refugee and displaced women
"Provide protection, assistance and training to refugee women, other displaced women in need of international protection and internally displaced women" (Strategic objective E.5)

States and other relevant actors, such as inter-governmental and non-governmental organizations, must:

- involve women in planning of refugee programmes, camps and resources (Paragraph 147a)
- make certain that refugee and displaced women and girls have direct access to services provided (Paragraph 147a)
- provide adequate protection from violence to such women both while displaced and on return to their homes (Paragraph 147b, c, d)
- provide rehabilitation to women in such circumstances (Paragraph 147c)
- thoroughly investigate any violence that does take place against refugee or displaced women (Paragraph 147c)

- ensure the right of refugee and displaced women to return in safety to their places of origin (Paragraph 147d)
- verify that the international community provides sufficient resources and relief to meet the needs of refugee and displaced women (Paragraph 147f)
- eliminate discrimination against women from the process of providing relief and assistance to refugees and displaced persons (Paragraph 147f)
- ensure equal access and treatment of women in refugee determination and asylum procedures (Paragraph 147h)
- consider recognizing as refugees those women whose claim to such status is based upon well-founded fear of persecution through sexual violence or other gender-related persecution (Paragraph 147h)
- provide women asylum-seekers access to specially trained personnel, including women officers, for interviews about experiences such as sexual assault (Paragraph 147h)
- spread awareness among refugee and displaced women of their rights (Paragraph 147k)
- provide women refugees with training programmes, counselling on violence against women, and rehabilitation programmes for all forms of torture and trauma (Paragraph 147l)
- contribute adequately to assistance for refugee women, both at the national and international levels (Paragraph 147l)
- promote public awareness of the situation of refugee women (Paragraph 147m)
- develop human rights education for military, security and police personnel and others working in refugee areas (Paragraph 147o)
- disseminate and follow the Guidelines on the Protection of Refugee Women of the UN High Commissioner for Refugees (UNHCR) (Paragraph 148a)

Assist women in non-self-governing territories
"Provide assistance to the women of the colonies and non-self-governing territories" (Strategic objective E.6)

The list of tasks for governments, intergovernmental and non-governmental organizations includes:

- supporting the right of self-determination (Paragraph 149a)
- promoting awareness of the situation of women in colonies and other non-self-governing areas (Paragraph 149b)

Status of the Beijing Platform for Action
Standards such as the Declaration on the Elimination of Violence against Women and the Beijing Platform for

Action show the repetition of obligations that suggest emerging norms of customary international law. Furthermore, in its Resolution 56/132, the UN General Assembly proposed a series of steps needed to "achieve full and accelerated implementation" of the Beijing Platform for Action (preamble).[143] The UN General Assembly "reaffirms the goals, objectives and commitments contained in the Beijing Declaration and Platform for Action" (Paragraph 1) and called upon governments, intergovernmental and non-governmental organizations "to take effective action to achieve full and effective implementation of the Beijing Declaration and Platform for Action". (Paragraph 3)

Specifically with regard to armed conflict, Resolution 56/132:

▶ recognizes the important role of women in conflict prevention and resolution, and in peace-building
▶ recognizes the importance of the equal participation of women in efforts to maintain peace and security (Paragraph 22)

UN Security Council Resolution 1325 (2000)

In 2000, the UN Security Council adopted Resolution 1325 on women, and peace and security.[144]

According to UN Charter Article 25, all UN members must "accept and carry out" Security Council resolutions. However, it should be noted that Resolution 1325 was not adopted under Chapter VII of the UN Charter, its most robust section, which covers action with respect to threats to the peace, breaches of the peace, and acts of aggression. This despite the fact that violence against women has been recognized as an obstacle to peace.

Reaffirming "the need to implement fully international humanitarian and human rights law that protects the rights of women and girls during and after conflicts" (Preamble), Resolution 1325 calls upon all member states to undertake the following tasks:

▶ ensure increased representation of women at all levels of decision-making, including in national, regional and international institutions which deal with conflicts (Paragraph 1)
▶ provide women candidates to the UN Secretary-General to be included in a centralized roster to increase the pool of qualified women available to the UN (Paragraph 3)
▶ incorporate gender training and HIV/AIDS awareness training into programmes for military and civilian police personnel who will participate in UN operations (Paragraph 6)
▶ increase their contributions and support for the UN's gender-sensitive training efforts (especially those of the UN Development Fund for Women (UNIFEM), and UNHCR. (Paragraph 7)

Through Resolution 1325, the Security Council calls on those actors involved in reaching peace agreements and implementing those agreements to adopt a gender perspective which:

▶ considers the needs of women and girls during repatriation, resettlement, rehabilitation, reintegration and reconstruction (Paragraph 8a)
▶ offers support for women's peace efforts and involvement of women in all implementation mechanisms (Paragraph 8b)
▶ ensures the protection of and respect for human rights of women and girls, especially in regards to the constitution, the electoral system, the judiciary and law enforcement (Paragraph 8c)
▶ factors in the needs of female ex-combatants and their dependants to any demobilization and reintegration strategies (Paragraph 13)

All parties to armed conflict are called upon to:

▶ respect fully international law applicable to the rights and protection of women and girls, especially as civilians. (Paragraph 9) The sources of that law explicitly mentioned include the 1949 Geneva Conventions and their 1977 Additional Protocols, the 1951 Refugee Convention and its 1967 Protocol, CEDAW and its optional protocol, and the CRC and its two optional protocols.
▶ "bear in mind the relevant provisions of the Rome Statute of the International Criminal Court" (Paragraph 9)

Resolution 1325 also includes an explicit appeal to all parties to armed conflict to:

▶ "take special measures to protect women and girls from gender-based violence, particularly rape and other forms of sexual abuse, and all other forms of violence in situations of armed conflict" (Paragraph 10)
▶ to respect the "civilian and humanitarian" character of refugee camps and settlements and use a

gender-sensitive methodology to design such facilities (Paragraph 12).

Resolution 1325 stresses the "responsibility of all States to put an end to impunity and to prosecute those responsible for genocide, crimes against humanity, and war crimes including those relating to sexual and other violence against women and girls". (Paragraph 11). It calls for these crimes to be excluded from amnesty provisions "where feasible". (Paragraph 11) While this provision has inherent weaknesses in comparison with

other Security Council actions on overcoming impunity, the resolution overall was a significant step for the Security Council in the gender area.

Resolution 1325 was adopted by a unanimous vote of the members of the Security Council which at the time included Argentina, Bangladesh, Canada, Jamaica, Malaysia, Mali, Namibia, Netherlands, Tunisia and Ukraine, as well as the permanent members (China, France, Russian Federation, United Kingdom and the USA).

9. Other relevant human rights standards

Universal Declaration of Human Rights

The Universal Declaration of Human Rights[145] is the founding document of the international human rights law structure. It states that recognition of "the equal and inalienable rights of all members of the human family is the foundation of... peace in the world". (Preamble)

The Universal Declaration of Human Rights guarantees many of the rights found in the International Covenant on Economic, Social and Cultural Rights and the International Covenant on Civil and Political Rights. It is particularly important in relation to those states that have not ratified those treaties and as a statement, at least in part, that is increasingly seen as reflecting customary international law.

In relevant articles it prohibits:

▶ sex discrimination (Articles 2 and 7)
▶ slavery and servitude (Article 4)
▶ torture or cruel, inhuman or degrading treatment or punishment (Article 5)
▶ arbitrary arrest, detention or exile (Article 9)

Of particular pertinence to women and girls in conflict, it guarantees:

▶ the right to life, liberty and security of person (Article 3)
▶ effective remedies from national tribunals for violations of rights (Article 8)
▶ fair trials (Articles 10, 11)

▶ freedom of movement, including the right to leave any country and to return to her country (Article 13)
▶ the right to seek asylum (Article 14)
▶ the right to marry in full equality and only with the free consent of spouses (Article 16(1), (2))
▶ protection for the family (Article 16)
▶ an adequate standard of living, including food and medical care (Article 25(1))
▶ special protection for motherhood and childhood (Article 25(2))
▶ the right to an education, particularly education that promotes peace (Article 26)

The Universal Declaration of Human Rights calls for these rights to be available at the national level, but also within the international context. "Everyone is entitled to a social and international order in which the rights and freedoms set forth in this Declaration can be fully realized." (Article 28) Moreover, it may be seen as being relevant to abuses by non-state actors since it proclaims itself as the "common standard of achievement for all peoples and all nations, to the end that every individual and every organ of society" shall strive to promote respect for these rights. (Preamble)

Vienna Declaration and Programme of Action

Women's rights are human rights. This basic pronouncement has its roots in the Vienna Declaration and Programme of Action which emerged from the World Conference on Human Rights in June 1993.[146] An entire section of the Programme of Action (Number 3) is devoted to "the equal status and human rights of women".

Governments are to make the "full and equal enjoyment by women of all human rights" a priority. (Paragraph 36) They are urged to eliminate violence against women "in public and private life" (Paragraph 38) in accordance with the provisions of the UN Declaration on the Elimination of Violence against Women (which had not yet been adopted). In particular, states should ratify CEDAW and should consider withdrawing their reservations to it. (Paragraph 39)

Specifically on women in conflict, the conference noted that:

"Violations of the human rights of women in situations of armed conflict are violations of the fundamental principles of international human rights and humanitarian law. All violations of this kind, including in particular, murder, systematic rape, sexual slavery, and forced pregnancy, require a particularly effective response." (Paragraph 38)

This ties in to the Declaration's general statement on armed conflicts which calls on "States and all parties to armed conflicts to observe humanitarian law... as well as minimum standards for protection of human rights, as laid down in international conventions". (Paragraph 29)

Cairo Declaration

The Cairo Declaration: The Programme of Action of the International Conference on Population and Development was adopted in 1994.[147] Women activists see the Cairo Declaration, along with the Vienna and Beijing pronouncements, as forming the bedrock of a new international vision for protecting women's human rights. A number of provisions are relevant to the protection of women from violence during and after armed conflict.

States are to:

▶ eliminate all practices that discriminate against women (Paragraph 4.4c)
▶ assist women in realizing their rights, including those related to reproductive and sexual health (Paragraph 4.4c)
▶ eliminate violence against women (Paragraph 4.4e)
▶ implement CEDAW, the Vienna Declaration and Programme of Action and the UN Declaration on Violence against Women (Paragraph 4.5)
▶ condemn rape, especially as a tool of war or form of ethnic cleansing, and provide women victims the means for full rehabilitation (Paragraph 4.10)

States must also take "collective measures" to alleviate the suffering of child victims of armed conflicts and to promote their rehabilitation. (Paragraph 6.12)

States should:

▶ provide reproductive health services for displaced persons that are sensitive to those who have been victims of sexual violence (Paragraph 7.11)
▶ engage in open discussion and education to address sexual abuse (Paragraph 7.39)
▶ strengthen the necessary laws (Paragraph 7.39)
▶ take the necessary steps to reduce maternal and infant mortality (Chapter VIII, B and C)

The document notes that internally displaced women may be at particular risk of rape and sexual assault and sets as an objective for states that they "offer adequate protection and assistance to persons displaced within their country, particularly women... and to find solutions to the root causes of their displacement". (Paragraph 9.20) Displaced women should receive training, health care, including reproductive care and family planning. (Paragraph 9.22) The Cairo Declaration also calls for effective security to be guaranteed to refugees, and for adequate provision to be made for their health, education and rehabilitation, in a gender-sensitive fashion. (Paragraph 10.22) Most fundamentally, governments are to respect refugee law and sign up to its provisions. (Paragraph 10.27)

Durban Declaration and Programme of Action

The Durban Declaration and Programme of Action emerged from the 2001 UN World Conference against Racism, Racial Discrimination, Xenophobia and Related Intolerance.[148] The Declaration flags racism and discrimination as frequent root causes of conflict. (Preamble) The Programme of Action goes on to call for respect for human rights and international humanitarian law in conflict situations, and to demand the peaceful resolution of disputes. (Paragraph 149) It urges the UN to work to "discern patterns of serious violations of human rights and humanitarian law with a view to assessing the risk of further deterioration that could lead to genocide, war crimes or crimes against humanity". (Paragraph 153) A specific call is made for states that have not done so to accede to the Geneva Conventions and their Additional Protocols, and to implement fully these rules in national legislation, especially those concerned with non-discrimination. (Paragraph 168)

Two

With particular reference to women, the Durban Declaration and Programme of Action draws international attention to the problem of overlapping discriminations and urges the integration of a gender perspective throughout the work of implementing its provisions. (Paragraph 50)

The Durban Declaration and Programme of Action urges states:

"(a) To recognize that sexual violence which has been systematically used as a weapon of war, sometimes with the acquiescence or at the instigation of the State, is a serious violation of international humanitarian law that, in defined circumstances, constitutes a crime against humanity and/or a war crime, and that the intersection of discrimination on grounds of race and gender makes women and girls particularly vulnerable to this type of violence, which is often related to racism, racial discrimination, xenophobia and related intolerance"

"(b) To end impunity and prosecute those responsible for crimes against humanity and war crimes, including crimes related to sexual and other gender-based violence against women and girls, as well as to ensure that persons in authority who are responsible for such crimes, including by committing, ordering, soliciting, inducing, aiding in, abetting, assisting or in any other way contributing to their commission or attempted commission, are identified, investigated, prosecuted and punished" (Paragraph 54)

UN Code of Conduct for Law Enforcement Officials

The Code of Conduct for Law Enforcement Officials[149] contains a number of principles of importance to the general protection of human rights. Those of particular relevance to protecting women from violence in conflict and post-conflict situations include:

- law enforcement officials shall respect and protect human dignity and human rights (Article 2)
- law enforcement officials may only use force when strictly necessary and in a strictly proportional fashion (Article 3)
- no law enforcement official may inflict or tolerate torture or other cruel, inhuman or degrading treatment or punishment, including in a state of war or public emergency (Article 5)
- law enforcement officials shall protect the health of people in their custody (Article 6)

UN Declaration of Basic Principles of Justice for Victims of Crime and Abuse of Power

The Declaration of Basic Principles of Justice for Victims of Crime and Abuse of Power[150] was adopted by the UN General Assembly in 1985. Article 1 of the Declaration defines a "victim" for these purposes as someone who has suffered harm through acts or omissions in violation of national criminal laws, including those laws that prohibit "criminal abuse of power". This would cover many abuses in armed conflict, particularly in internal conflict.

The Declaration states that victims should:

- be treated with respect for their dignity (Paragraph 4)
- have access to justice and prompt redress (Paragraph 4)
- be informed of their rights to redress (Paragraph 5)
- receive necessary medical and other assistance (Paragraph 14)
- have access to health and social services (Paragraph 15)
- be offered restitution, where appropriate, including for harms committed by state agents in which case such restitution must come from the state (Paragraphs 8 and 11)
- be assisted in a way that does not discriminate on the basis of, among other things, sex. (Paragraph 3)

When compensation is not available from other sources, states should compensate victims, or their surviving family members, who have "sustained significant bodily injury or impairment" as a result of serious crimes. (Paragraph 12) Implicitly, the Declaration encourages the creation of international funds to assist in this process, noting that there may be circumstances in which the victim's home state "is not in a position to compensate the victim". (Paragraph 13)

Police, justice and other personnel who may work with victims should receive special training. All services and assistance should take into account any special needs of victims based on the nature of the harm they have suffered or based on a series of factors, including sex. (Paragraphs 3 and 17)

"Victims of abuse of power" have suffered harm due to violations of international law, which may not yet be violations of the relevant domestic law. They are also to receive support and assistance and states are to consider offering them compensation and restitution. States should pass laws proscribing serious abuses of power and should develop the remedies available to such victims. (Paragraphs 18 to 21)

Recommendations of UNIFEM independent experts

Ellen Johnson Sirleaf, a Liberian woman activist and former government minister, and Elisabeth Rehn, a former Finnish minister of defence and UN Under-Secretary-General, were commissioned in April 2001 as independent experts by UNIFEM (the United Nations Development Fund for Women). They were asked to undertake a worldwide study of the impact of war on women. They took a holistic approach to the subject, considering women's health in conflict, gender-sensitive justice and reconstruction, women refugees and the role of the media. They have put forward a set of recommendations on violence against women in conflict.[151] Although these are recommendations, rather than a binding legal text, as the expert recommendations of two women with such backgrounds published through the UN system, they should be seen as significant.

With regard to conflict violence against women, they suggest the following:

▶ setting up an international truth and reconciliation commission on violence against women as a step towards ending impunity
▶ targeted sanctions against trafficking of women and girls in and through conflict zones, avoiding prosecution of the victims of trafficking
▶ recognition of domestic violence as a systematic and widespread problem in conflict and post-conflict situations which needs to be addressed in any humanitarian, legal or security response and in training for those involved in emergencies and reconstruction.
▶ governments and other actors such as donors and the UN should provide long-term support for women survivors of violence, including legal, economic, psychosocial and reproductive health services.[152]

Other general human rights standards

A number of other general human rights standards may be consulted with regard to protecting women in time of armed conflict. These include:

▶ The UN Principles on the Effective Prevention and Investigation of Extra-legal, Arbitrary and Summary Executions

▶ The Declaration on the Rights of Disabled Persons
▶ The Basic Principles on the Use of Force and Firearms by Law Enforcement Officials
▶ The Declaration on the Protection of All Persons from Enforced Disappearance
▶ The International Convention on the Protection of the Rights of All Migrant Workers and Members of Their Families
▶ The Declaration on the Elimination of All Forms of Intolerance and of Discrimination Based on Religion or Belief
▶ The Standard Minimum Rules for the Treatment of Prisoners
▶ The Body of Principles for the Protection of All Persons under Any Form of Detention or Imprisonment
▶ The Declaration on the Protection of All Persons from Being Subjected to Torture and Other Cruel, Inhuman or Degrading Treatment or Punishment
▶ The Principles on the Effective Investigation and Documentation of Torture and Other Cruel, Inhuman or Degrading Treatment or Punishment
▶ The Principles of Medical Ethics relevant to the Role of Health Personnel, Particularly Physicians, in the Protection of Prisoners and Detainees against Torture and Other Cruel, Inhuman or Degrading Treatment or Punishment
▶ The Safeguards guaranteeing protection of the rights of those facing the death penalty

All of these texts are available on the website of the UN High Commissioner for Human Rights at www.ohchr.org/english/law/index.htm. The recommendations of the Special Rapporteurs of the Commission on Human Rights, in particular the Special Rapporteur on violence against women, and the human rights treaty bodies, should also be consulted.

Women and post-conflict situations

Women face a range of problems in post-conflict environments that may lead to violence. In some cases the environment is even worse for them than during the conflict. Problems include:

▶ an increase in polygamy, owing to death of the husband
▶ difficulty of remarriage
▶ loss of social position
▶ high suicide rates among victim-survivors, especially of sexual violence

- loss of any "advantages" women may have gained during conflict, for example the return of newly or previously abusive partners, and women's removal or retreat from new roles in the public sphere, especially employment
- the creation of female-headed households, often impoverished due to discrimination
- an increase in prostitution and trafficking, especially related to peacekeepers and aid workers
- financial burdens for survivors of violence, especially sexual violence and forced pregnancy (abortion or adoption or child raising, plus medical care)
- non-eligibility for pensions

In recent years, there has been growing awareness of the disturbing fact that peacekeepers and aid workers, sent by the international community to support affected populations in such times, might actually be perpetrators of abuses against women, especially in post-conflict situations. This has largely been in the field of sexual harassment and sexual violence, and participation in trafficking and using the services of prostitutes. Most peacekeepers and aid workers play a constructive and important role in post-conflict countries. However, the involvement of international community personnel in abuses against women must be confronted. The UN has developed codes of conduct for its personnel in the field which include prohibitions on sexual abuse or exploitation of local women. UN Secretary-General Kofi Annan announced a UN policy of "zero tolerance" for such abuses and issued a special bulletin in October 2003 entitled "Special measures for protection from sexual exploitation and sexual abuse".[153] These policies and codes must be fully implemented as a matter of priority.

Standards governing the post-conflict phase in particular are very limited. Human rights experts are working on draft legislation (a Penal Code and Code of Criminal Procedure) which can be used in post-conflict justice systems, based on lessons learned in situations like Kosovo and Cambodia. In the meantime, the UN system has adopted another document which may be of use. It focuses on the responsibilities of the UN, an important beginning to addressing this aspect of conflict.

The Windhoek Declaration

The Windhoek Declaration (The Namibia Plan of Action on "Mainstreaming a Gender Perspective in Multidimensional Peace Support Operations") was adopted at a seminar organized by the UN Department of Peacekeeping Operations (DPKO) on 31 May 2000.[154] This standard addresses vital issues of sexual assault and harassment in post-conflict countries, the prevention of trafficking in women and the way in which women's human rights evolve in the post-conflict society. It also addresses the question of whether those who have perpetrated violence against women during the conflict are brought to justice and victim-survivors compensated.

As the preamble to the Windhoek Declaration says:

"In order to ensure the effectiveness of peace support operations, the principles of gender equality must permeate the entire mission, at all levels, thus ensuring the participation of women and men as equal partners and beneficiaries in all aspects of the peace process – from peacekeeping, reconciliation and peace-building, towards a situation of political stability in which women and men play an equal part in the political, economic and social development of their country."

To this end, the Declaration urges the following:

1. Negotiations and peace agreements
- women should be equal participants in ceasefire and peace talks
- gender issues should be fully addressed in any such agreements

2. Mandate
- gender issues and perspectives and the provisions of CEDAW, in particular, should be fully integrated in any UN peace support mission from beginning to end and explicitly included in any relevant Security Council resolution

3. Leadership
- more women must be appointed to relevant high-ranking UN posts, such as Special Representatives of the Secretary-General and senior field staff
- all senior personnel should receive in-depth briefing on gender issues

4. Planning, structure and resources of missions
- effective, adequately resourced gender affairs units should be standard features of all UN missions
- all UN Department of Peacekeeping Operations (DPKO) planning teams and briefings must include gender specialists and cover gender issues
- gender mainstreaming should be prioritized in terms of allocation of resources, and updated based on lessons learned from each past mission

5. Recruitment

▶ member states should increase their female personnel in military and police forces contributed to UN missions

▶ all personnel sent to the field should have gender issues explicitly addressed in their contracts

6. Training

▶ all personnel contributed to UN missions should receive gender training and many women should be involved as trainers

▶ mandatory gender training should be given upon arrival at mission area, addressing:
▷ code of conduct
▷ culture, history and social norms of host country
▷ CEDAW
▷ sexual harassment and sexual assault

7. Procedures

▶ a Senior Gender Adviser post should be created and fully funded in the DPKO

gender issues need to be fully incorporated into DPKO directives, reporting mechanisms and internal communications

▶ standard operating procedures need to be developed on the issues of sexual assault and sexual harassment

8. Monitoring, evaluation and accountability

▶ accountability for these recommendations should be at the highest levels

▶ reporting, evaluation and research should be encouraged

9. Public awareness

▶ all possible means should be used to spread public awareness of the centrality of gender issues in peace support operations

The UN Secretary-General is to ensure the achievement of these tasks, but "in consultation with Member States", who can do a great deal to ensure their realization.

Two

Part Three: INTERNATIONAL HUMANITARIAN LAW

10. The laws of war

Another body of law is applicable to women in war – international humanitarian law, the law which regulates the conduct of hostilities and the treatment of civilians, prisoners of war, and others specially affected in cases of armed conflict. International human rights law and international humanitarian law should be thought of as working in tandem in conflict situations.

In times of armed conflict, the international community turns to international humanitarian law as a way to lessen the human cost of war and to supplement human rights law. The International Committee of the Red Cross (ICRC) is recognized in the Geneva Conventions and other instruments as a guardian of international humanitarian law, overseeing and facilitating its implementation. It may offer its services to parties to conflict in a range of ways, such as helping to care for the wounded and sick, facilitating the creation and recognition of hospital zones, and assisting prisoners of war.

The Geneva Conventions and their Additional Protocols

The core of contemporary international humanitarian law consists of the four Geneva Conventions of 1949 and their two Additional Protocols of 1977. Each treaty has a somewhat different focus and less protection is afforded by this body of treaty law in internal conflict than in international conflict.

The four Geneva Conventions of 1949 are:

▶ Geneva Convention for the Amelioration of the Condition of the Wounded and Sick in Armed Forces in the Field[155] (First Geneva Convention, or Geneva I)
▶ Geneva Convention for the Amelioration of the Condition of Wounded, Sick and Shipwrecked Members of Armed Forces at Sea[156] (Second Geneva Convention, or Geneva II)
▶ Geneva Convention Relative to the Treatment of Prisoners of War[157] (Third Geneva Convention, or Geneva III)
▶ Geneva Convention Relative to the Protection of Civilian Persons in Time of War[158] (Fourth Geneva Convention, or Geneva IV). Experts have argued that this Convention is potentially the most relevant for women because they are generally civilians in time of war.

A total of 192 states are now parties to these treaties.[159] The bulk of each of the Conventions applies only in cases of *international* armed conflict.

Common Article 3, found in all four of the Conventions, also applies in cases of "armed conflict not of an international character", i.e. internal conflict, that takes place on the territory of a state party. Among other things, it requires that "persons taking no active part in the hostilities" be treated humanely, without discrimination on the basis of, among other things, sex.

The Protocols Additional to the 1949 Geneva Conventions that were adopted in 1977 are:

► **Protocol Additional to the Geneva Conventions of 12 August 1949, and Relating to the Protection of Victims of International Armed Conflicts[160] (Protocol I)**

This treaty supplements and clarifies the rules from 1949 governing international conflicts, in particular with regard to shielding the civilian population from the effects of hostilities. As a product of the time in which it was drafted, which coincided with decolonization, it further extends its protections to those conflicts "in which peoples are fighting against colonial domination and alien occupation and against racist régimes in the exercise of their right of self-determination". (Article 1(4)) There are currently 162 state parties to Protocol I.[161]

► **Protocol Additional to the Geneva Conventions of 12 August 1949, and Relating to the Protection of Victims of Non-International Armed Conflicts[162] (Protocol II)**

Despite the breadth of its title, Protocol II in fact only applies to a limited subset of internal, non-international armed conflicts: those occurring in the territory of a state party between the forces of the state and *armed groups which exercise control over territory* and have *responsible command*, such that they are able to fulfil the provisions of the Protocol. (Article 1) Therefore, only conflicts involving armed groups which have a high level of organization and which have gained control of territory are covered by Protocol II. This Protocol supplements the protections found in common Article 3 of the four Geneva Conventions, but does not apply to the full range of conflicts covered by that article. Furthermore, the wording of the Protocol specifically excludes situations of "internal disturbances and tensions, such as riots, isolated and sporadic acts of violence and other acts of a similar nature". (Article 1(2))[163] There are currently 157 states parties to Protocol II.[164]

Customary international law – the Martens clause

In addition to their treaty obligations, states and other parties to the conflict are bound by rules of customary international humanitarian law.[165] Customary rules of international humanitarian law may be found in military manuals and treaties, some of them dating back to the 19th century, but also in the Geneva Conventions and Additional Protocols themselves, many of whose provisions are widely considered to reflect customary rules.[166]

One important customary provision is the so-called Martens clause, which made its first appearance in the preamble to the 1899 Hague Convention (II) with respect to the laws and customs of war on land. It is named after the Russian law professor, von Martens, who composed it.[167] The clause was restated, in one form or another, in all of the Geneva Conventions and their Additional Protocols, where it provides that even if a state decides to "denounce" any of those treaties, such denunciation,

"shall in no way impair the obligations which the Parties to the conflict shall remain bound to fulfil by virtue of the principles of the law of nations, as they result from the usages established among civilized peoples, from the laws of humanity and the dictates of the public conscience."[168]

In other words, the Martens clause reminds parties to a conflict that there are basic principles which should guide their conduct regardless of the nature of the conflict or the precise language of treaty provisions. The prohibition of violence against women may safely be considered as one of these basic principles.

Caution required in interpreting international humanitarian law

International humanitarian law must be interpreted carefully. Each treaty has a specific scope of application, in terms of the kinds of situations to which it applies and the categories of person to whom it offers protection. Most of the provisions apply only once a conflict has begun, although some, particularly those regarding dissemination of information about international humanitarian law and military training, apply also in peacetime.[169]

The four Geneva Conventions cease to apply at the close of hostilities, for the most part, except in occupied territory where many of the provisions of the Fourth Geneva Convention remain in effect until a year after the end of military operations (see Article 6, Geneva IV).[170] However, the Occupying Power is bound, "for the duration of the occupation", by many of the Convention's provisions, including, for instance, the provision that civilians in the hand of an Occupying Power must "at all times be humanely treated". (Article 27) Protocol I applies fully to situations of occupation until the occupation ends.[171] In internal armed conflict, under Protocol II, those articles specific to the protection of detained persons (Articles 5 and 6) continue to protect individuals detained related to the conflict until they are freed.[172]

Common Article 1: 'respect and ensure respect' for humanitarian law

The obligation to "respect and to ensure respect" for humanitarian law in all circumstances is found in Article 1 common to all four Geneva Conventions. This Article provides that "[T]he High Contracting Parties undertake to respect and to ensure respect for the present Convention in all circumstances."[173] According to the ICRC Commentary on Article 1, this is a "fundamental principle."[174] The same language is used in Article 1 of the two 1977 Protocols (with the substitution of "Protocol" for "Convention".)

As the ICRC Commentary on the Geneva Conventions further notes:

"The Contracting Parties do not undertake merely to respect the Convention, but also 'to ensure respect' for it. The wording may seem redundant. When a State contracts an engagement, the engagement extends *eo ipso* [by that very act] to all those over whom it has authority, as well as to the representatives of its authority; and it is under an obligation to issue the necessary orders. The use of the words 'and to ensure respect' was, however, deliberate: they were intended to emphasize and strengthen the responsibility of the Contracting Parties. It would not, for example, be enough for a State to give orders or directives to a few civilian or military authorities, leaving it to them to arrange as they pleased for the details of their execution... It is for the State to supervise their execution. Furthermore, if it is to keep its solemn engagements, the State must of necessity prepare in advance, that is to say in peacetime, the legal, material or other means of loyal enforcement of the Convention as and when the occasion arises."[175]

Professors Laurence Boisson de Chazournes and Luigi Condorelli have described the meaning of common Article 1 as follows:

"The obligation to respect and to ensure respect for humanitarian law is a two-sided obligation, for it calls on States both 'to respect' and 'to ensure respect' the Conventions [sic]. 'To respect' means that the State is under an obligation to do everything it can to ensure that the rules in question are respected by its organs as well as by others under its jurisdiction. 'To ensure respect' means that States, whether engaged in a conflict or not, must take all possible steps to ensure that the rules are respected by all, and in particular by parties to conflict."[176]

This means that the state not only has to refrain from committing abuses, but it must also protect those under its jurisdiction or control from abuses by others, such as private actors, vital in the area of women's human rights.

Commonly, this was understood to refer largely to the responsibilities of states, whether or not they were parties to a particular conflict, to ensure that the Conventions were respected in any conflict between state parties or in any occupation involving them. However, it is clearly a broad enough engagement of responsibility to refer also to a state protecting women within its territory from whatever the source of violations of the Conventions. This is made explicit in Protocol 1, Article 86, which requires punishment of violations of the Conventions or Protocols which "result from a failure to act when under a duty to do so".

Furthermore, the International Court of Justice stated in the *Nicaragua* case that the obligation to "respect" and "ensure respect" in common Article 1 "does not derive only from the Conventions themselves, but from the general principles of humanitarian law to which the Conventions merely give specific expression." In other words, it is a norm of customary international law binding on all states.[177]

Substantive obligations

Women are theoretically to benefit, just as men are supposed to, from the general protections offered by international humanitarian law. They should be protected by provisions shielding combatants and those who are not, or are no longer, combatants: the wounded, shipwrecked, prisoners, and civilians (including internees) when they fit into each of those categories.[178] While women and girls do sometimes serve as combatants, a reality which must not be overlooked, they most often fit into the category of civilians. Therefore, the Fourth Geneva Convention which protects civilians in time of war or occupation, and the analogous provisions covering internal armed conflict, are seen as particularly relevant to their situation.

In addition to the general provisions of international humanitarian law, there are some which are gender-specific. According to the ICRC, some 50 out of 560 articles of the Conventions and Protocols deal with non-discrimination or otherwise provide "special protection for women".[179]

Three

Non-discrimination

The 1949 Geneva Conventions and the 1977 Protocols establish a principle of equality to the effect that "no *adverse* distinction can be drawn between individuals on the basis of, *inter alia*, sex."[180] This principle is reflected, for example, in Article 12 of the Second Geneva Convention which requires humane treatment of people in the power of parties to the conflict. It prohibits "any adverse distinction founded on sex... or any other similar criteria" in such treatment. Article 2(1) of Protocol II repeats this language with respect to the internal armed conflicts that it covers.

Note that it is only *adverse* distinctions which are banned, and as the experts Judith Gardam and Michelle Jarvis conclude, "differentiation on the basis of sex is thus permissible as long as its impact is favourable."[181] For example, sex may be considered, as well as several other factors, in determining if labour is appropriate for a particular prisoner of war (Geneva III, Article 49) or the quality and quantity of bedding and blankets for internees in occupied territory (Geneva IV, Article 85) or the appropriateness of a disciplinary penalty for an internee in occupied territory (Geneva IV, Article 119). The commentary on the Fourth Geneva Convention suggests the need for a careful approach:

"Equality might easily become injustice if it was applied to situations which were essentially unequal, without taking into account such circumstances as the... sex of the protected persons concerned."[182]

Common Article 3 – basic considerations of humanity

Article 3, found in all four Geneva Conventions, is unique within those Conventions in that it also applies in cases of "armed conflict not of an international character", i.e. internal conflict, that takes place on the territory of a state party. As such, it obligates "each Party to the conflict" rather than states alone.

Among other things, it protects "persons taking no active part in the hostilities" by prohibiting the following practices (sub-paragraph 1):

"a. violence to life and person, in particular murder of all kinds, mutilation, cruel treatment and torture

b. taking of hostages

c. outrages upon personal dignity, in particular humiliating and degrading treatment

d. the passing of sentences and the carrying out of executions without previous judgment pronounced by a regularly constituted court"

It requires that people taking no active part in the hostilities "shall in all circumstances be treated humanely," without discrimination on the basis of, among other things, sex (Sub-paragraph 1), and that "the wounded and sick shall be collected and cared for". (Sub-paragraph 2)

The International Court of Justice has determined, in the *Nicaragua* case, that common Article 3 reflects fundamental general principles of humanitarian law.[183] It added that "in the event of international armed conflicts, these rules also constitute a minimum yardstick" of conduct for parties to the conflict.[184] The International Criminal Tribunal for the former Yugoslavia added that common Article 3 is "applicable to armed conflicts *in general*."[185] (Emphasis added.)

It should also be noted that Article 75 of Protocol I and Article 4 of Protocol II offer similar "fundamental guarantees" for the humane treatment of non-combatants.

11. 'Special protection' for women

A set of interrelated provisions set out the basic approach of the Geneva Conventions and their Additional Protocols to the safeguarding of women in conflict.

These general provisions are seen as the touchstone of the protection of women under Geneva law, although standing alone they do not entail specific obligations.[186] They are supplemented by specific provisions detailed below. The goal of these rules, taken together, has been described as "to either reduce the vulnerability of women to sexual violence, to directly prohibit certain types of sexual violence, or to protect them when pregnant or as mothers of young children."[187]

"Women shall be treated with all consideration due to their sex." (Article 12, First and Second Geneva Conventions)

The ICRC Commentary suggests that this provision is "an example of a favourable distinction made compulsory".[188] As to the meaning of this provision, the Commentary which was published in 1960 by the ICRC explains as follows: "What special consideration? No doubt that accorded in every civilized country to beings who are weaker than oneself and whose honour and modesty call for respect." [189] This language, and the view of women that under-pins it, has been criticized by feminist scholars of international humanitarian law.[190] However, the key notion of respect can be extracted from this old-fashioned interpretation.

"Women shall be treated with all the regard due to their sex and shall in all cases benefit by treatment as favourable as that granted to men." (Article 14, Third Geneva Convention)

This article refers to women prisoners of war. According to the ICRC Commentary, the key points to be taken into consideration in deciphering the meaning of this provision are: "(a) weakness; (b) honour and modesty; (c) pregnancy and child-birth".[191] "Weakness", though an unfortunate word choice in retrospect, seems to refer to women's physical capacity, which is to be considered with regards to working conditions they are to face and food they must receive. The concern with "honour and modesty" is an archaic way of expressing the intention to protect women from sexual abuse. Thirdly, special treatment should be afforded to pregnant women and mothers of babies and young children (specifics detailed below). In short, women must be treated at least as well as men and in some ways more favourably.

The ICRC Commentary reflects the necessity of considering women's particular circumstances in interpreting Geneva law as a whole, not just where this issue is explicitly flagged.

"Does this privilege cover all the provisions of the Convention or, on the contrary, does it only refer to those provisions which make express reference to it? In our view, this reference tends to strengthen the scope of the principle rather than to limit it."[192]

The dictate of Article 14 is specifically noted in the ICRC Commentary as being relevant to the protection of prisoners from public curiosity and insults, provisions for food and clothing and conditions for transfer, among others. However, sex is not explicitly mentioned in the relevant articles.

"Women shall be especially protected against any attack on their honour, in particular against rape,

enforced prostitution, or any form of indecent assault." (Article 27, Fourth Geneva Convention)

The ICRC Commentary interprets this specific obligation as arising from the general concern for women's honour and family rights, but also for respect for their person. In that regard, they are entitled to special protection, in addition to the ordinary safeguards which shield them along with men. The Commentary expresses outrage at the sexual atrocities against women committed during the Second World War (which were inadequately prosecuted afterwards), followed by a broad condemnation, as follows:

"These acts [rape, enforced prostitution and any form of indecent assault] are and remain prohibited in all places and in all circumstances, and women, whatever their nationality, race, religious beliefs, age, marital status or social condition have an absolute right to respect for their honour and their modesty, in short, for their dignity as women."[193]

Protocol 1 asserts a similar rule: **"Women shall be the object of special respect and shall be protected in particular against rape, forced prostitution and any other form of indecent assault."** (Protocol 1, Article 76, from Chapter II – "Measures in Favour of Women and Children")

Women in detention and internment

In addition to the general provisions for the protection of all women, women who are detained or imprisoned in connection with a conflict[194] are to be afforded particular treatment:

▶ separate dormitories and conveniences must be provided for women prisoners of war[195] (even during disciplinary punishment) and women internees (except when interned along with a family unit) and other women detainees (Geneva III, Articles 25, 29, 97; Geneva IV, Article 85; Protocol II, Article 5(2)(a))

▶ female supervision is required for female prisoners of war under disciplinary punishment (under Geneva III) and at all times (under Protocol 1); as well as for women internees and detainees, including those in occupied territory (except when held with a family unit) (Geneva III, Article 97; Geneva IV, Article 76; Protocol I, Article 75(5); Protocol II, Article 5(2)(a))

▶ women internees are only to be searched by women (Geneva IV, Article 97(4)); in interpreting the gender-specific provisions of the Geneva system, the ICRC

has written more broadly that women detainees should be searched by women personnel only[196]

▶ a female prisoner of war cannot be sentenced or punished in a more severe way than a female member of the armed forces of the detaining power would be. Furthermore, a woman prisoner of war may in no case be "awarded or sentenced to a punishment more severe, or treated whilst undergoing punishment more severely, than a *male* member of the armed forces of the Detaining Power dealt with for a similar offence" (emphasis added) (Geneva III, Article 88)

▶ pregnant women and mothers with dependent infants "who are arrested, detained or interned for reasons related to the armed conflict, shall have their cases considered with the utmost priority" (Protocol 1, Article 76(2))

▶ extra provision of food is to be made, as needed, to interned expectant and nursing mothers (Geneva IV, Article 89)

Mothers and pregnant women

Pregnant women and so-called maternity cases are often "assimilate(d)... to the sick and wounded" in Geneva law, as the expert Françoise Krill notes.[197] Such women are afforded special protection, usually, but not exclusively, under this rubric.

▶ mothers and pregnant women should receive special treatment in regards to medical care (Geneva IV, Article 91)

▶ hospitals (and their personnel and land and air vehicles) for the care of wounded and, *inter alia*, "maternity cases" must be protected and respected; they may in "no circumstances be the object of attack" (Geneva IV, Articles 18, 20, 21 and 22)

▶ states must allow free passage of foodstuffs and supplies to pregnant women and nursing mothers (Geneva IV, Article 23)

▶ detaining powers must supply extra provisions of food, as needed, to interned expectant and nursing mothers (Geneva IV, Article 89)

▶ pregnant women and nursing mothers are to be given priority in the distribution of relief supplies (Protocol I, Article 70)

▶ states parties are to consider the possibility of establishing safety zones for, among others, pregnant women and mothers with children under seven (Geneva IV, Article 14)

▶ parties should endeavour to evacuate "maternity cases," namely women about to give birth or in the process of giving birth, from conflict zones (Geneva IV, Article 17)

▶ attempts should be made at early repatriation, release or accommodation in a neutral country for interned pregnant women and mothers with infants and young children, among others (Geneva IV, Article 132)

▶ maternity cases among internees in occupied territory must be admitted to medical facilities where they may receive adequate care; that care must be the same as that available to the population at large (Geneva IV, Article 91)

▶ maternity cases among internees should not be transferred if this would be detrimental to their health, unless their safety so requires (Geneva IV, Article 127)

▶ as aliens and in occupied territory, pregnant women and mothers of children under seven are to be accorded the same preferential treatment as those categories among nationals of that state. (Geneva IV, Article 38) According to the ICRC Commentary, this may include preferential treatment in regards to "the granting of supplementary ration cards, facilities for

medical and hospital treatment, special welfare treatment, exemption from certain kinds of work, protective measures against the effects of war, evacuation, transfer to a neutral country, admission to hospital and safety zones and localities, etc."[198]

▶ occupying powers cannot alter preferential measures for pregnant women and mothers of children under seven that were in effect prior to the occupation (Geneva IV, Article 50)

▶ the death penalty is "to the maximum extent feasible" not to be imposed on pregnant women or those with dependant infants for an offence related to the conflict; in any case such sentences are not to be carried out (Protocol 1, Article 76(3))

▶ death sentences are not to be carried out on pregnant women in internal armed conflict (Protocol II, Article 6(4))

▶ as noted above, pregnant women and mothers with dependent infants "who are arrested, detained or interned for reasons related to the armed conflict, shall have their cases considered with the utmost priority" (Protocol 1, Article 76(2))

12. International humanitarian law prohibiting gender-specific abuses

Prevention of rape and other sexual abuse

"Women shall be especially protected against any attack on their honour, in particular against rape, enforced prostitution, or any form of indecent assault." (Geneva IV, Article 27) This provision protects women from harm committed by agents of states of which they are not nationals during international armed conflict and occupation.

"Women shall be the object of special respect and shall be protected in particular against rape, forced prostitution and any other form of indecent assault." (Protocol I Article 76(1)) This applies to all women in the territory of parties to an international conflict or in occupied territory, within the scope of Protocol I

"[T]he following acts against... [persons taking no part in the hostilities] are and shall remain prohibited at any time and in any place whatsoever: ...outrages upon personal dignity, in particular humiliating and degrading treatment, rape, enforced prostitution and any form of indecent assault" (Protocol II, Article 4(2)) This applies to women in non-international armed conflict.

A similar rule against "outrages upon personal dignity" is found in Protocol 1. However, it prohibits "in particular humiliating and degrading treatment, enforced prostitution and any form of indecent assault" without specific mention of rape. (Protocol I, Article 75(2)(b)) Nevertheless, given the language of Protocol II quoted immediately above, this must be read by implication to include rape as a form of outrage on personal dignity. Furthermore, threats to commit such abuses are also absolutely forbidden. (Protocol I, Article 75(2)(e))

The ICRC Commentary to Geneva III, Article 14, weaves together a number of specific provisions of that Convention, making clear that they are aimed at preventing sexual assaults on women prisoners of war. These include providing separate housing (Article 25), sanitary installations (Article 29) and differential execution of punishment for women prisoners (Articles 97 and 108). Additionally, this encompasses provisions protecting prisoners in general from insults and public curiosity (Article 13(2)), limiting the nature of questioning and interrogation (Article 17) and requiring adequate clothing to be provided (Article 27).

Prohibition of rape and other sexual violence during conflict

Rape and other sexual abuse by state officials or with their instigation, consent or acquiescence, and in detention, or by organized armed groups, constitute torture or ill-treatment. Rape and sexual abuse of women in such contexts – as in any context – also clearly constitute forms of violence against women. Therefore, a number of other provisions of Geneva law may be considered, by implication, to outlaw these practices. (Some of these are of particular legal significance in relation to grave breaches of international humanitarian law, see below). These provisions include:

In international armed conflict:

- the wounded and sick on land and sea and the shipwrecked must be respected, protected and treated humanely; protected from violence and torture (Geneva I and II Article 12)
- enemy civilians must not commit violence against the wounded and sick covered by the treaty (Geneva I, Article 18)
- prisoners of war must be treated humanely, "physical mutilation" is prohibited, as are "acts of violence or intimidation", insults and exposure to public curiosity. "Any unlawful act or omission by the Detaining Power causing death or seriously endangering the health of a prisoner of war... is prohibited and will be regarded as a serious breach of the present Convention." (Geneva III, Article 13)
- prisoners of war are entitled to respect "for their persons and their honour" (Geneva III, Article 14)
- "Women shall be treated with all the regard due to their sex" (Geneva III, Article 14)
- prisoners of war may not be tortured, coerced, threatened, or insulted in interrogation (Geneva III, Article 17)
- protected persons are entitled to respect for their persons, honour, and family rights, and to be humanely treated and protected from violence (Geneva IV, Article 27)
- state parties may take no measure that causes physical suffering of protected persons. They must not commit acts of torture, mutilation or "any other measures of brutality whether applied by civilian or military agents" (Geneva IV, Article 32)
- "torture of all kinds, whether physical or mental" of persons in the power of a party to the conflict is prohibited (Protocol I, Article 75(2)(a)(ii))

- mutilation (must be read to include sexual mutilation) is prohibited (Protocol I, Article 75(2)(a)(iv))

In internal armed conflict:

- torture, mutilation and other forms of violence are prohibited (Protocol II, Article 4(2)(a))
- the wounded, sick and shipwrecked shall be collected and cared for, respected, protected nd treated humanely (Protocol II, Articles 7, 8)
- individual civilians shall not be subject to attack. Acts or threats of violence for the primary purpose of spreading terror among the civilian population shall not be tolerated (Protocol II, Article 13)
- people not taking a direct part in the hostilities shall be treated humanely and in a non-discriminatory fashion. They are entitled to respect for their person and honour (Protocol II, Article 4(1))
- violence to the health and physical or mental well-being of people, cruel treatment, torture and mutilation are forbidden (Protocol II, Article 4(2)(a))
- "slavery and the slave trade in all their forms" are prohibited (Protocol II, Article 4(2)(f))

Common Article 3 contains the following provisions relevant to the prohibition of rape and other sexual violence:

- Common Article 3 (1)(a) prohibits violence to the person including "mutilation, cruel treatment and torture"
- Common Article 3 (1)(c) prohibits "outrages upon personal dignity, in particular humiliating and degrading treatment"

13. Abuses that disproportionately affect women

The Beijing Platform for Action notes that "Civilian victims, mostly women and children, often outnumber casualties among combatants."[199] Gardam and Jarvis have argued that the legal principle of Geneva law which is most important for women during the conduct of hostilities is that of non-combatant immunity.[200] This principle is a cornerstone of international humanitarian law. It requires parties to the conflict to distinguish between civilians (and other non-combatants) and combatants at all times and to refrain from targeting civilians and other non-combatants.

This principle, also known as the principle of distinction, is a norm of customary international humanitarian law. It does not, unfortunately, amount to a total prohibition on *killing or injuring* civilians. Parties to a conflict must distinguish civilians and other non-combatants from combatants. They must only target combatants, but they are not prohibited from launching an attack on military targets, knowing that *some* civilians will be killed, subject to the principles of necessity and proportionality.

Protocol I offers detailed rules (Articles 48 to 58) for how this is to be implemented (in international and self-determination related conflicts). It may therefore be seen as particularly important for women.

Protocol I, Article 51 prohibits:

▶ direct attacks on civilians
▶ acts with the primary purpose of spreading terror among civilians
▶ reprisals against civilians
▶ using civilians as a shield for military operations
▶ indiscriminate attacks

Indiscriminate attacks are:

▶ those not specifically targeting a particular military objective
▶ those which employ an inherently indiscriminate method or means, such as an indiscriminate weapon
▶ those which treat a group of military targets, which may be separated by civilian areas, as one target

Article 51(5)(b) also elaborates the crucial principle of proportionality. This prohibits:

"an attack which may be expected to cause incidental loss of civilian life, injury to civilians, damage to civilian objects, or a combination thereof, which would be excessive in relation to the concrete and direct military advantage anticipated."

Many of these vital provisions are also thought to constitute norms of customary international law, and therefore binding on states that are not party to Protocol I. However, this issue is hotly contested, for example by official representatives of the USA, the only permanent member of the UN Security Council not to have ratified this Protocol. The USA recognizes many of the provisions but not all as reflecting customary international law.

In non-international armed conflict, the most common form in our time, the rules governing the means and methods of combat have not been very well developed, leaving women and others particularly vulnerable. Protocol II, Article 13, provides general norms to protect the civilian population from the effects of conflict.

Protocol II, Article 13 prohibits:

▶ direct targeting of civilians
▶ the use of acts of violence or threats thereof to terrorize the civilian population.

However, as Gardam and Jarvis have noted:

"...Protocol II contains no specific limitations on the means and methods of combat. There is no prohibition against indiscriminate attacks or any requirement as to proportionality, no prohibition on the civilian population being used as a shield against military operations, and no prohibition against reprisals."[201]

However, it is safe to state that the prohibitions on targeting civilians and indiscriminate attacks, the requirement of proportionality and the prohibition on reprisals against civilians are norms of customary international law as regards non-international and internal conflicts as well as international ones.[202] The norms in Geneva law regulating the conduct of internal armed conflict should be understood in the context of existing and developing customary rules in the area. The Rome Statute of the International Criminal Court has made a further significant contribution in this regard (see below).

14. Grave breaches of the Geneva Conventions and Protocol I

Violations of Geneva law may be divided into grave breaches, specifically enumerated in the four Geneva Conventions and in Protocol I, and other acts contrary to the provisions of the Conventions. Protocol II does not make distinctions between different violations. Parties to the Conventions and Protocol I are to "take measures necessary for the suppression of" *any* contravention of the rules, whether considered a grave breach or not.[203]

With regard to grave breaches, all state parties must:

▶ enact laws that give rise to individual criminal responsibility for grave breaches of international humanitarian law (for both those who have ordered and those who have committed such breaches)
▶ criminalize such conduct and the ordering of such conduct
▶ search for the alleged perpetrators (including those who gave the orders)
▶ exercise jurisdiction over such alleged perpetrators by bringing them before its courts in trials in accordance with humanitarian law protections for defendants
▶ or turn them over to another state that will do so

Furthermore, no state may excuse itself or any other from legal responsibility for the commission of grave breaches. Experts have decried the fairly universal failure to live up to these standards with regard to most allegations of grave breaches, including those committed against women.

There is no explicit reference to gender-based abuses in the list of grave breaches found in the four Geneva Conventions and Protocol I. However, the torture of women is clearly a grave breach of these treaties, and this undoubtedly includes rape and many other forms of sexual abuse, such as sexual mutilation. A number of other provisions of particular relevance to violence against women in wartime are included.

Grave breaches

The following provisions define grave breaches:

Geneva I, Article 50; Geneva II, Article 51; Geneva III, Article 130:

▶ includes "torture or inhuman treatment" and "wilfully causing great suffering or serious injury to body or health" of protected persons

Geneva IV, Article 147:

▶ contains the same relevant provisions as those above, but also includes others which may be of particular concern with regard to gender-based abuses (like sexual slavery and trafficking in women) such as unlawful deportation or transfer, and unlawful confinement of a protected person

Protocol I, Article 85:

▶ contains the same relevant provisions as those above, but also refers to making the civilian population or individual civilians the object of attack (85(3)(a)); launching an indiscriminate attack knowing this will cause excessive loss to civilians (85(3)(b)); attacking a person knowing that person is hors de combat (85(3)(e)); transfer (85(4)(a))

Protocol II contains no provisions defining grave breaches, but serious violations of Protocol II are war crimes under the statutes of the International Criminal Tribunal for the former Yugoslavia, the International Criminal Tribunal for Rwanda, the International Criminal Court, the Special Court for Sierra Leone and the International Panels for East Timor. They are also criminalized widely in national legislation.

War crimes

What does the expression "war crime" mean? A war crime is "a violation of the laws and customs of war" which is of a certain level of seriousness. The term "war crime" only appears once in the Geneva Conventions.[204] Protocol I, however, states that grave breaches of its terms or those of the four Geneva Conventions constitute war crimes. (Article 85(5)) In addition, serious violations of the Geneva Conventions and Protocol I not explicitly specified as grave breaches may still constitute war crimes and therefore entail international criminal responsibility.

The Rome Statute of the International Criminal Court (Article 8(2)) (see below) names and punishes certain offences that fit in this category (serious violations of international humanitarian law not explicitly designated grave breaches including rape, sexual slavery, enforced prostitution, forced pregnancy and enforced sterilization). Still, the Geneva Conventions and Protocol I themselves place a lower level of responsibility on states for the suppression of these other war crimes and violations than for those explicitly recognized as grave breaches.

15. Responsibilities of armed groups under international humanitarian law

International humanitarian law, especially common Article 3 and Additional Protocol II, also applies to the actions of armed groups. Common Article 3, which specifically provides that "each Party to the conflict" is bound by its provisions, obviously applies to armed groups. While Additional Protocol II, like other international humanitarian law treaties, is an agreement between "High Contracting Parties", Article 1(1) provides that the Protocol applies to situations where a state is fighting "dissident armed forces or other organized armed groups." State practice affirms that armed groups are seen as bound by both of these standards as groups, in addition to the provision of individual responsibility for group members.[205] (For a summary of the obligations detailed in Protocol II and common Article 3, see above.) This has been supported by the International Court of Justice in the *Nicaragua* case[206] and the Inter-American Commission on Human Rights in the *Tablada* case with regards to common Article 3.[207] In the latter case, the Inter-American Commission noted that,

"Common Article 3's mandatory provisions expressly bind and apply equally to both parties to internal conflicts, i.e., government and dissident forces. Moreover the obligation to apply Common Article 3 is absolute for both parties and independent of the obligation of the other."[208]

The UN Commission on Human Rights has also called on armed groups to observe Protocol II.[209]

The relevance of the provisions is without regard to the consent of the armed groups in question, unlike states which have the sovereign right to decide whether to ratify a treaty or not. In fact, some armed groups have tried to adhere officially to international humanitarian law

treaties, a practice which has usually been opposed by governments.[210] In any case this is not explicitly permitted under the terms of these treaties, although special arrangements, like those used in the former Yugoslavia, are encouraged. Armed groups are bound by the international humanitarian law treaties ratified by the state on whose territory they operate.

A separate mention must be made of "national liberation movements," a set of groups to whom Protocol I may apply. The exact definition of such groups is difficult to apply, but in the terms of the Protocol, includes those:

"fighting against colonial domination and alien occupation and against racist regimes in the exercise of their right of self-determination, as enshrined in the Charter of the United Nations and the Declaration on Principles of International Law concerning Friendly Relations and Co-operation among States in accordance with the Charter of the United Nations."[211]

Such groups are allowed to make a declaration to the effect that they will be bound by the Conventions and Protocol I.[212]

In addition to international humanitarian law treaties, customary international law binds armed groups. As seen above, Common Article 3 of the Geneva Conventions has been recognized as reflecting customary international norms. As such, the rules in Common Article 3 are applicable to all parties to all conflicts, regardless of ratification of the Geneva Conventions. This is largely a non-issue due to the widespread, although not universal, ratification of the four

Conventions. On the other hand this is very much a live issue with regard to Protocol II. Aspects of this more detailed but less widely applicable standard have been invoked as customary norms by the International Criminal Tribunal for the former Yugoslavia, the International Criminal Tribunal for Rwanda and the Inter-American Commission on Human Rights. The UN Commission on Human Rights has gone so far as to cite Protocol II in relation to armed groups in states that are not parties to Protocol II.

Hence, these specified provisions of international humanitarian law can and should be used to hold armed groups responsible for their often grave and systematic violence against women in armed conflict. The procedures of international criminal law bolster accountability in this area.

Three

Part Four: INTERNATIONAL CRIMINAL LAW

16. International criminal law

Early international criminal law codes penalized gender-based abuses both in international and non-international armed conflict. They were included in the Lieber Code of 1863 (section 44),[213] and in the list prepared in 1919 by the Commission on Responsibilities,[214] and were cited at the Versailles Peace Conference of 1919. These early codes were inadequate in their coverage of gender-based crimes and failed to enforce restitution, although other, more general provisions were thought to cover such offences. For example, the London Charter that created the Nuremberg Tribunal after the Second World War did not mention the offence of rape. However, Control Council Law No. 10, which served as the basis for prosecuting some low-level Nazi officials, did list rape as a crime against humanity.[215]

The Tokyo War Crimes Tribunal did charge rape as an offence but used one of the Hague Regulations[216] covering "family honour" as the basis for such prosecutions. Furthermore, it utterly failed to confront the horror of the systematic sexual slavery practiced by the Japanese military.[217] This situation has been greatly ameliorated, particularly during the 1990s with the renaissance of international criminal law.[218]

Ad hoc international criminal tribunals

The International Criminal Tribunal for the former Yugoslavia (1993) and the International Criminal Tribunal for Rwanda (1994) were set up by the UN Security Council to address violations of international law in these two country situations.[219] In their statutes, rape is listed as among the crimes against humanity, when part of an attack on a civilian population, within the tribunals' jurisdiction. In practice, the jurisprudence of these two tribunals has recognized rape and other forms of sexual abuse as "among the most serious" of offences and they have been "charged and prosecuted as such".[220] For example, rape and other forms of sexual violence have been prosecuted as constitutive elements of genocide, torture and other inhumane acts.[221]

Rape, enforced prostitution and indecent assault are explicitly included in the statute of the International Criminal Tribunal for Rwanda[222] as violations of common Article 3 and Protocol II.

The International Criminal Tribunal for Rwanda has, in the case of *Akayesu*, found an accused guilty of rape for failing, as an official, to prevent or stop rape, rather than for personally raping. The Tribunal considered rape to amount to torture[223] and, in the circumstances, found mass rape, as part of "measures intended to prevent births within the group," to constitute an act of genocide.[224]

In the cases of *Akayesu*[225] and *Celebici*, rape was identified specifically as an act of torture when perpetrated by or at the instigation of a public official, and in the case of *Furundzija*, when it takes place during interrogation. In the case of *Kunarac et al* (known as *Foca*),[226] the defendants were convicted of rape as a crime against humanity and rape as a violation of the laws and customs of war (under Article 3 common to the Geneva Conventions).

The tribunals convicted men of acts such as sexual enslavement, forced nudity and sexual humiliation – in addition to rape and sexual assault – thus recognizing such acts as serious international crimes.

The *ad hoc* tribunals addressed the impunity of members of armed forces and also of civilians. The tribunals confirmed that breaches of Common Article 3 of the Geneva Conventions are war crimes. This means that members of armed groups, as well as members of official armies, can be held criminally responsible for their acts.

The rules of procedure and evidence of the tribunals, particularly of the International Criminal Tribunal for the former Yugoslavia, also made advances in addressing violence against women. While conscious of the need to protect defendants' rights, the sensitivities of victims and witnesses were a significant concern. To protect those willing to testify from the shame and stigma so often associated with rape, and from being targeted for new attacks by their assailants or others, the rules permitted the use of pseudonyms; allowed voices and photographic images to be electronically disguised; and agreed that transcripts could be edited to remove any reference to victims' identities.[227]

Other customary difficulties in sexual assault cases, which are also common to such cases in peacetime, were addressed. Sexual assaults and rape are often defined in terms of specific physical parts. For example, rape is defined in many jurisdictions as penetration of a vagina by a penis. The many different types of sexual attack, such as forced oral sex and insertion of objects into women's bodies, cannot be covered by such a restrictive definition. In the *Akayesu* case, the concept of "invasion" was developed, defining rape as "a physical invasion of a sexual nature".[228] This line of development was pursued so that the definition of rape as a crime against humanity for the International Criminal Court reflects it. Article 7(1)(g) (1) of the Elements of Crimes defines one element of the crime of rape thus: "The perpetrator invaded the body of a person by conduct resulting in the penetration however slight, of any part of the body of the victim or of the perpetrator with a sexual organ, or of the anal or genital opening of the victim with any object or any other part of the body."

The *Akayesu* case defined rape as taking place in "circumstances which are coercive" and this line of reasoning has been used in many cases since. This is important, as international law recognizes that in situations of armed conflict, normal ideas of consent to sexual relationships cannot be seen as applying, given the circumstances of coercion and fear of violence.[229]

In many jurisdictions, it is difficult for a woman to persuade the court that she did not consent to sex, which usually leads to a finding that she was not raped and the acquittal of the perpetrator. In the tribunals, consent was not allowed as a defence if the victim had been subjected to, threatened with, or had reason to fear duress, detention or psychological oppression, or believed that if she did not submit, another person might be assaulted, threatened or put in fear.

The prior sexual conduct of the victim is frequently brought to the attention of courts to imply that she would be more likely to agree to sex and less likely to have been raped. The rules of procedure of the International Criminal Tribunal for the former Yugoslavia do not allow evidence of prior sexual conduct to be admitted as evidence.

The Tribunals were innovative and responsive to women's needs in recommending protective measures for victims and witnesses. They provided counselling and support for them, particularly in cases of rape and sexual assault. Support units for victims and witnesses were established by both tribunals, mandated to adopt a gender-sensitive approach and give due consideration to the appointment of qualified women gender specialists.

International Criminal Court

Thanks to the efforts of the women's human rights movement, in particular the Women's Caucus for Gender Justice, as well as Amnesty International and other human rights organizations, gender-based offences are specifically enumerated in the Rome Statute of the International Criminal Court (1998).[230] They are therefore explicitly included within the jurisdiction of the International Criminal Court. These include rape, sexual slavery, enforced prostitution, forced pregnancy, enforced sterilization and "other forms of sexual violence". These acts are criminalized as crimes against humanity, Article 7(1)(g); as war crimes in international armed conflict, Article 8(2)(b)(xxii), and as war crimes in non-international armed conflict, Article 8(2)(e)(vi)). The crime of sexual slavery received its first treaty recognition, and trafficking in persons was recognized as a form of enslavement for the first time.

Gender-based persecution of groups is criminalized in Article 7(1)(h), and enslavement, including "the exercise of such power in the course of trafficking in persons, in particular women and children"[231] in Article 7(1)(c). Both of these practices are considered crimes against humanity.

The International Criminal Court Rules of Procedure and Evidence built on achievements of the tribunals

Four

regarding principles of evidence, in camera procedures, witness and victim protection, and gender sensitivity. The International Criminal Court was also empowered to award reparations. The need to ensure a "fair representation" of female and male judges was acknowledged,[232] as well as to appoint experts in sexual and gender violence as staff in the Registry and Office of the Prosecutor. The election of seven women judges in February 2003 will hopefully be a step in that direction.

Major progress has been made in setting up the International Criminal Court since the entry into force of the Rome Statute on 1 July 2002. Ninety-seven states – almost half the international community – have ratified the Rome Statute, committing themselves to investigate and prosecute people accused of genocide, crimes against humanity and war crimes in their national courts.[233] The International Criminal Court will step in only when national courts are unable or unwilling to do so.

On 23 June 2004, following a referral by the government of the Democratic Republic of the Congo, the International Criminal Court Prosecutor announced the opening of the court's first investigation into "serious crimes" committed in the Democratic Republic of the Congo. This investigation will include crimes against humanity and war crimes such as murder, rape and torture that were committed after the International Criminal Court's jurisdiction began on 1 July 2002.

It is to be hoped that when the International Criminal Court begins its important work of prosecuting the most serious offences in the world, it will give thorough attention to violence against women in conflict.

Four

Part Five: INTERNATIONAL REFUGEE LAW

17. International and regional refugee law

Refugee law is another body of international law that is important to women caught in armed conflict. International refugee law is closely connected to human rights law and international humanitarian law. Its role is to address the situation whereby an individual is forced to flee his or her country of origin to seek international protection as a result of fearing or suffering violations of basic human rights. The distinct problem of internal displacement, or dislocation within the borders of one's own country, is discussed below. According to the UN High Commissioner for Refugees (UNHCR), 75 to 80 per cent of the world's refugees and internally displaced persons are women and children, making standards in these areas crucial for women's rights advocates.

Refugee treaties

The 1951 Convention and 1967 Protocol relating to the Status of Refugees are the principal international instruments dealing with the plight of refugees.[234] The 1951 Convention relating to the Status of Refugees (Refugee Convention)[235] sets out the definition of a refugee as well as the standards of treatment that are to be accorded to refugees. The Convention's applicability was universalized through the adoption of the 1967 Protocol relating to the Status of Refugees which removed the geographical and time limitations contained in the Refugee Convention.[236]

Article 1A(2) of the Refugee Convention defines a refugee as:

"any person who...owing to well-founded fear of being persecuted for reasons of race, religion, nationality, membership of a particular social group or political opinion, is outside the country of his [or her] nationality and is unable or, owing to such fear, is unwilling to avail himself [or herself] of the protection of that country..."

The definition of a refugee requires that a person is outside his or her country and therefore does not cover internally displaced persons. (For discussion of standards related to internal displacement, see below.) The Refugee Convention's focus on civil or political status as being the reason for persecution means that refugees fleeing situations of generalized violence or conflict or serious disturbances of public order may not fall within the scope of the Convention.[237]

Regional standards

Two regional instruments provide a broader scope of refugee protection than that explicitly stipulated in the Refugee Convention: the 1969 Organization for African Unity Convention Governing the Specific Aspects of Refugee Problems in Africa;[238] and the 1984 Cartagena Declaration on Refugees. Both instruments take the Refugee Convention as their starting point and expand the Convention's definition of a refugee to take account of other causes of flight including generalized violence, internal conflicts, massive violations of human rights, external aggression, occupation or foreign domination.

Refugee law and gender

The Refugee Convention does not include any specific references to gender or the situation of women fleeing armed conflict in search of international protection. A gender-inclusive and gender-sensitive interpretation of the Convention's provisions is however required on the basis of the Convention's text, object and purpose.[239] Whereas gender is not an independently enumerated ground for Convention protection, developments in state practice and case law since the 1990s have contributed to a greater recognition of the protection needs of refugee women. Gender-related claims have been recognized by many states as being within the ambit of the "social group" category of the Refugee Convention. Gender has also been increasingly recognized as an important factor when looking into claims based on any of the other Convention grounds. Forms of gender-related violence, including sexual violence, have further been acknowledged as being persecution within the meaning of the Refugee Convention, including when committed by non-state actors.

The Refugee Convention makes no direct references to the concept of asylum or the conditions under which it is to be granted. Rather, it provides for the principle of *non-refoulement*. It stipulates in Article 33 that:

"no Contracting State shall expel or return ('*refouler*') a refugee in any manner whatsoever to the frontiers of territories where his [or her] life or freedom would be threatened..."

Article 3 of the 1984 Convention against Torture, Article 7 of the International Covenant on Civil and Political Rights, and Article 3 of the European Convention for the Protection of Human Rights and Fundamental Freedoms have also been invoked to provide protection from *refoulement* based on the danger of being subjected to torture. The principle of *non-refoulement* has been widely recognized as a rule of customary international law and therefore binding on all states independently of assent to specific treaties.

Non-treaty standards relating to refugee women

The Conclusions of the Executive Committee (EXCOM) of the UN High Commissioner for Refugees (UNHCR) describe state consensus on important protection policies and practices and set international protection standards.[240]

Although not binding in nature, states are expected to pay "due regard" to EXCOM Conclusions when meeting their protection obligations.[241] EXCOM has adopted a number of Conclusions that refer to the specific situation and problems of refugee women. They include a number of recommendations for appropriate measures to be taken to guarantee protection from violence, threats to physical safety or exposure to sexual abuse or harassment.[242]

Among the Conclusions of UNHCR's Executive Committee, 1993 EXCOM Conclusion No. 73 (XLIV) and 2003 EXCOM Conclusion No. 90 (LIV) deal specifically with refugee protection and sexual violence and protection from sexual abuse and exploitation. They urge states to adopt and implement concrete measures to prevent and combat sexual violence and exploitation including: the development and implementation of training programmes targeting law enforcement officers and members of the military; implementation of effective, non-discriminatory legal remedies for victims of sexual violence; and activities aiming at empowering refugee women and other vulnerable groups and enhancing their participation in decision-making processes.

Practical advice to all those involved in international protection activities is provided by UNHCR's *Guidelines on the Protection of Refugee Women*[243] and *Sexual and Gender-based Violence against Refugees, Returnees and Internally Displaced Persons: Guidelines for Prevention and Response*.[244] The latter document provides an overview of root causes and consequences of sexual-based violence. It makes recommendations on: prevention strategies; working with children subjected to or at risk of sexual and gender-based violence; establishing multi-sectoral response systems; and setting up evaluation mechanisms for measuring the impact of actions designed to protect against sexual and gender based violence. It also explains the concept of gender-related persecution and how to apply it when working with asylum-seekers. This is an area addressed in detail by UNHCR's *Guidelines on International Protection: Gender-Related Persecution within the context of Article 1A (2) of the 1951 Convention and/or its 1967 Protocol relating to the Status of Refugees*.[245] Guidance on how to address problems of sexual and gender-based violence is further provided in the *Inter-agency Field Manual on Reproductive Health in Refugee Situations* produced by the World Health Organization (WHO), the UN Population Fund (UNFPA) and UNHCR.[246]

In 2001, the UNHCR made five commitments to refugee women, aimed at improving their legal and material protection and assistance. UNHCR offices are to incorporate these commitments in their work. They

Five

include a recognition that "sexual and gender-based violence continues to be a severe impediment to the advancement of women and the enjoyment of their rights" and a commitment to developing integrated country-level strategies to address such violence.[247]

Internally displaced persons

The Refugee Convention definition of a refugee requires that a person be outside his or her country, and therefore does not cover internally displaced persons. Nevertheless, by analogy, refugee law and UNHCR guidance can be useful when establishing guidelines or standards of protection for internally displaced persons, given the similarities in the experiences of refugees and the internally displaced. UNHCR policy has also direct application in situations where the UNHCR has been called to act on behalf of internally displaced persons in certain situations at the request of the UN General Assembly or the UN Secretary-General.

The UN Guiding Principles on Internal Displacement,[248] based upon existing international humanitarian law and human rights norms, set out the international standards for providing assistance and protection to internally displaced persons. These are to guide the work of governments and international organizations working with the internally displaced. According to this standard, internally displaced persons are those:

"who have been forced or obliged to flee or to leave their homes or places of habitual residence, in particular as a result of or in order to avoid the effects of armed conflict, situations of generalized violence, violations of human rights or natural or man-made disasters, and who have not crossed an internationally recognized border."

Principle 11 is of relevance to protection from gender-related violence. This refers to the right to dignity and physical, mental and moral integrity and sets out the obligation to provide protection against:

"(a) rape, mutilation, torture, cruel, inhuman or degrading treatment or punishment, and other outrages upon personal dignity, such as acts of gender-specific violence, forced prostitution and any form of indecent assault; (b) slavery or any contemporary form of slavery, such as sale into marriage, sexual exploitation, or forced labour of children; and (c) acts of violence intended to spread terror among internally displaced persons."

Furthermore, Principle 19 provides for special attention to be paid to the health needs of women, including "appropriate counselling for victims of sexual and other abuses".

In the application of all of the Guiding Principles on Internal Displacement, discrimination on the basis of sex is explicitly prohibited (Principle 4(A)). Furthermore, expectant mothers, mothers with young children and female heads of household are explicitly "entitled to protection and assistance required by their condition and to treatment which takes into account their special needs." (Principle 4(B))

18. Is new international law needed to protect women in armed conflict?

The official position of the ICRC is that sufficient rules exist in international humanitarian law to prevent violence against women in armed conflict. However, the real problem is the failure to implement this law. According to the ICRC, "If women have to bear so many of the tragic effects of conflict, it is not because of any shortcomings in the rules protecting them, but because those rules are not observed."[249] It repeatedly calls on governments to respect and implement existing rules.

Françoise Krill wrote in 1985 that:

"If women in real life are not always protected as they should be, it is not due to the lack of a legal basis... The international community will not succeed in remedying this situation merely by adopting new rules. Most of all, it must see that the rules already in force are respected."[250]

A number of contemporary feminist critics disagree and suggest that the language of the rules of international humanitarian law regarding women, especially as reflected in the Commentaries on the Geneva Conventions, is archaic and reflects stereotypical ideas about women that perpetuate discrimination and hence violence itself.[251] Furthermore, Gardam and Jarvis have concluded that it is "apparent from a comparison between the reality of armed conflict for women... and the existing relevant norms of international law, that the latter are inadequate." [252]

They suggest several possible strategies to address this problem. One is the approach of law reform in the specific form of a new treaty on women and armed conflict. Another is the reinterpretation of existing provisions with a gender perspective.[253] These authors recognize the political difficulties potentially involved in a new treaty drafting exercise, given the need to preserve existing norms of international humanitarian law which some states might like to weaken. However, in noting the plethora of standards which have been produced in this field in recent years, they suggest the possibility of a comprehensive instrument to draw these together. In their view, this could take the form of a UN General Assembly resolution or Guiding Principles on Women and Armed Conflict, inspired by the analogous standard prepared on Internal Displacement.[254]

Another idea which has garnered widespread support is the updating of the Commentaries on the Geneva Conventions and Protocols from a fully gender-sensitive perspective. This could be prepared as a supplement that does not undermine the existing ICRC Commentaries. This idea has been endorsed by the Special Rapporteur on violence against women and by non-governmental organizations. All of these approaches could be important steps towards greater protection for women in war. However, any such effort would need to be balanced with a great emphasis on full and universal implementation of existing rules which would go a long way towards the protection of women in conflict.

Six

19. Conclusions

This report has sought to outline the main principles of international law applicable to violence against women in armed conflict and to review the principal international instruments which codify it.

Pre-conflict situations, conflicts and post-conflict situations are complex. Different strands of international law apply in a sometimes overlapping and often confusing way to different situations.

It is important to keep in mind, however, that basic considerations of humanity apply to all conflicts, as do the non-derogable provisions of international human rights law and any other human rights law which has not actually been derogated from. The basic considerations of humanity are provided for in international humanitarian treaty rules which reflect customary international legal norms. In effect both humanitarian and human rights law unite to form one overarching set of legal rules. Violence against women is prohibited at all times, in all its forms, by all strands of international law discussed here. Acts of violence against women constitute violations of non-derogable human rights when perpetrated by state officials, or when states fail to exercise due diligence to protect women and girls from violence by non-state actors. Such forms of violence, as well as gender-based abuses by armed groups, may also constitute breaches, including grave breaches, of international humanitarian law; and they also constitute crimes under international criminal law, where such violence is extensive or particularly severe.

Pointing to the exact legal provisions breached in a particular circumstance may be straightforward, but making states and armed groups apply these provisions is much more difficult. Amnesty International hopes that this report will assist women survivors of violence, and any person advocating for or working with women victims of violence, to use the law to secure justice and remedies for women.

Six

1 International Women's Rights Project, *The First CEDAW Impact Study*, June 2000. Available at http://www.iwrp.org/CEDAW_Impact_Study.htm, p. 15.

2 For stylistic reasons, Amnesty International sometimes uses the term "war", although legal standards refer to "armed conflict".

3 UN Declaration on the Elimination of Violence against Women, General Assembly resolution 48/104 of 20 December 1993, UN Doc. A/RES48/49, 1993. Available at http://www.unhchr.ch/huridocda/huridoca.nsf/(Symbol)/A.RES.48.104.En?Opendocument.

4 Committee on the Elimination of Discrimination Against Women, General Recommendation 19, Violence against women, (11th Session, 1992) UN Doc. HRI\GEN\1\Rev.1. Available at http://www.un.org/womenwatch/daw/cedaw/recommendations/recomm.htm#recom19.

5 Vann, Beth, *Gender-Based Violence: Emerging Issues in Programs Serving Displaced Populations*, 2002, p. 8. Available at http://www.rhrc.org/resources/gbv/

6 UN Security Council resolution 1325 on Women and Peace and Security, adopted 31 October 2000. UN Doc. S/RES/1325, 2000, preamble. Available at: www.un.org/News/Press/docs/2001/SC6988.doc.htm.

7 The case of an internally displaced woman in Liberia. Cited in, Rehn, Elisabeth, and Sirleaf, Ellen J., *Women, War, Peace, The Independent Experts' Assessment of the Impact of Armed Conflict on Women and Women's Role in Peace-building*, UN Development Fund for Women (UNIFEM), 2002, p. 32.

8 *Mejía v. Peru*, Report No. 5/96, Case 10.970, 1 March 1996, Inter-American Commission on Human Rights, "Facts Reported". Available at www.cidh.oas.org/women/Peru10970.eng.htm.

9 Filipina former "comfort woman" Maxima Regala Dela Cruz, subjected to sexual slavery by the Japanese military, explains the treatment she and others endured during the Second World War. Cited in *Summary of Findings of the Women's International War Crimes Tribunal 2000 for the Trial of Japanese Military Sexual Slavery*, 12 December 2000, para 2.

10 Report of the UN Special Rapporteur on violence against women, its causes and consequences, Violations against women perpetrated and/or condoned by the State during times of armed conflict (1997-2000), UN Doc. E/CN.4/2001/73, para. 101. Available at http://documents-dds-ny.un.org/doc/UNDOC/GEN/G01/104/44/PDF/G0110444.pdf?OpenElement.

11 Bennoune, Karima, "'A Disease Masquerading as a Cure': Women and Fundamentalism in Algeria, An Interview with Mahfoud Bennoune," in Reed, Betsy (ed.), *Nothing Sacred: Women Respond to Religious Fundamentalism and Terror*, Nation Books, 2002, p. 84.

12 Sources from which this list has been compiled include, Gardam, Judith and Jarvis, Michelle, "Women and Armed Conflict: The International Response to the Beijing Platform for Action", Vol. 32, *Columbia Human Rights Law Review* 1, 2000, 12-14; Gardam, Judith and Jarvis, Michelle, *Women, Armed Conflict and International Law*, Kluwer Law International, 2001; and Rehn, Elisabeth, and Sirleaf, Ellen J., *Women, War, Peace, The Independent Experts' Assessment of the Impact of Armed Conflict on Women and Women's Role in Peace-building*, UNIFEM, 2002.

13 For example, Agent Orange.

14 For example, depleted uranium weapons.

15 Lindsay, Charlotte, *Women Facing War: ICRC study on the impact of armed conflict on women*, ICRC, 2001, p. 24.

16 Obligations *erga omnes* are those obligations which, by their nature, a state holds to the entire international community, such as the prohibitions of genocide and slavery. Such obligations "are the concern of all States," and "all States can be held to have a legal interest in their protection…" *Case Concerning the Barcelona Traction, Light and Power Company, Limited (New Application 1962) (Belgium v. Spain)* [1970] ICJ Rep. 4 at paras 33-34. This means that any state has the right to protest. See also, Steiner, Henry and Alston, Philip, *International Human Rights in Context: Law, Politics, Morals*, Oxford University Press, 2000, pp. 224-25, 234.

17 See for example, Schmeidl, Susanne, and Piz-Lopez, Eugenia, *Gender and Conflict Early Warning: A Framework for Action*, International Alert, 2002.

18 For example, see discussion in Charlesworth, Hilary and Chinkin, Christine, *The Boundaries of International Law: A Feminist Analysis*, Manchester University Press, 2000, p. 273.

19 See Charlesworth, Hilary, and Chinkin, Christine, *The Boundaries of International Law*, Manchester University Press, 2000, pp. 160, 166; *Lives blown apart, Crimes of violence against women in times of conflict*, Amnesty International (AI Index: ACT 77/075/2004).

20 Additional Protocol II to the Geneva Conventions, Article 1 (2).

21 See, for example, Knop, Karen "Re/Statements: Feminism and State Sovereignty in International Law," 3 *Transnational Law and Contemporary Problems* 292, 1993; Charlesworth, Hilary, and Chinkin, Christine, *The Boundaries of International Law: A Feminist Analysis*, Manchester University Press, 2000; Dallmeyer, Dorinda (ed.), *Reconceiving Reality: Women and International Law*, American Society of International Law, 1993; Chinkin, Christine: "A gendered perspective to the International Use of Force", *Australian Year Book of International Law*, 1988; Gardam, Judith, and Jarvis, Michelle, "Women in Armed Conflict: The International Response to the Beijing Platform for Action", Vol. 32 *Columbia Human Rights Law Review* 1, 2000.

22 Crimes against humanity are defined in the Rome Statute of the International Criminal Court as any of the following acts when committed as part of a widespread or systematic attack directed against any civilian population, with knowledge of the attack: Murder; Extermination; Enslavement; Deportation or forcible transfer of population; Imprisonment or other severe deprivation of physical liberty in violation of fundamental rules of international law; Torture; Rape, sexual slavery, enforced prostitution, forced pregnancy, enforced sterilization, or any other form of sexual violence of comparable gravity; Persecution against any identifiable group or collectivity on political, racial, national, ethnic, cultural, religious, gender or other grounds that are universally recognized as impermissible under international law; Enforced disappearance of persons; The crime of apartheid; Other inhumane acts of a similar character intentionally causing great suffering, or serious injury to body or to mental or physical health.

23 Genocide is defined in the Convention on the Prevention and Punishment of Genocide as any of the following acts committed with intent to destroy, in whole or in part, a national, ethnical, racial or religious group, as such: Killing members of the group; Causing serious bodily or mental harm to members of the group; Deliberately inflicting on the group conditions of life calculated to bring about its physical destruction in whole or in part; Imposing measures intended to prevent births within the group; Forcibly transferring children of the group to another group.

24 Customary international law is derived from two elements: 1) state practice and 2) *opinio juris*, a subjective element based on the state's view that the practice in question was required by law.

Each element must be sufficiently established to show the existence of a particular customary international law principle.

25 General principles of law must be used in a vast majority of the world's legal systems, and across types of legal systems. They are most often used with regard to procedural matters and to fill gaps in existing international law.

26 Vienna Convention on the Law of Treaties, Article 53. The Vienna Convention on the Law of Treaties is available at http://www.un.org/law/ilc/texts/treaties.htm.

27 http://www.unhchr.ch/tbs/doc.nsf/Statusfrset?OpenFrameSet.

28 See *Making rights a reality: The duty of states to address violence against women*, Amnesty International (AI Index: ACT 77/049/2004), Chapter 4, Due diligence.

29 Reservations are defined by Article 2(1)(d) of the Vienna Convention on the Law of Treaties.

30 See Articles 19-23. The Vienna Convention on the Law of Treaties is available at http://www.un.org/law/ilc/texts/treaties.htm. Note that the rules governing reservations to human rights treaties are the subject of considerable controversy. But the continuing validity of the Vienna Convention framework has recently been affirmed by the UN expert body, the International Law Commission.

31 See *Making rights a reality: The duty of states to address violence against women*, Amnesty International (AI Index: ACT 77/049/2004), Chapter 8, Reparation.

32 See *Making rights a reality: The duty of states to address violence against women*, Amnesty International (AI Index: ACT 77/049/2004).

33 Special Rapporteur on violence against women, Report to the Commission on Human Rights, UN Doc. E/CN.4/2003/75, 2003, para. 85.

34 Preliminary report submitted by the Special Rapporteur on violence against women, its causes and consequences, UN Doc. E/CN.4/1995/42, 1994, para 72.

35 *Velázquez-Rodríguez v. Honduras*, Inter-American Court of Human Rights (series C), July 29, 1988, No. 4, para 172.

36 For a discussion of Amnesty International's approach to "due diligence" vis-à-vis women's human rights, see *Respect, protect, fulfil: Women's human rights – State responsibility for abuses by "non-state actors"*, Amnesty International (AI Index: IOR 50/001/2000).

37 Preliminary report submitted by the Special Rapporteur on violence against women, its causes and consequences, UN Doc. E/CN.4/1995/42, 1995, para. 72.

38 Center for Women's Global Leadership, "Statement to 57th Session of the Commission on Human Rights", 10 April 2001. Available at www.cwgl.rutgers.edu/globalcenter/policy/2001chrstatement.html.

39 See *Respect, protect, fulfil: Women's human rights – State responsibility for abuses by "non-state actors"*, Amnesty International (AI Index: IOR 50/001/2000).

40 The text of CEDAW is available at: http://www.ohchr.org/english/law/cedaw.htm. Entered into force 2 September 1981.

41 Committee on the Elimination of Discrimination against Women, General Recommendation No. 19, Violence against women, (11th Session, 1992) UN Doc. HRI\GEN\1\Rev.1. Available at http://www.un.org/womenwatch/daw/cedaw/recommendations/recomm.htm#recom19.

42 See Vienna Convention on the Law of Treaties, Article 18. Note that the Vienna Convention's provisions are largely considered to reflect customary international law, which is important for those states, such as the USA, which have not ratified the Vienna Convention on the Law of Treaties either. Hence, their treaty practice is in many ways still governed by its rules.

43 The Protocol entered into force on 22 December 2000. Available at: http://www.unhchr.ch/html/menu3/b/opt_cedaw.htm

44 The Optional Protocol entered into force on 22 December 2000. Available at http://www.unhchr.ch/html/menu3/b/opt_cedaw.htm.

45 As of 28 February 2005.

46 CRC, Article 1. Note, however, that Article 1 qualifies this by saying that it applies to all such persons "unless under the law applicable… majority is attained earlier." Of course the CRC applies to both boys and girls. In this report, the focus is only on girls. The CRC is available at www.ohchr.org/english/law/crc.htm. Entered into force 2 September 1990.

47 UNICEF, *Implementation Handbook for the Convention on the Rights of the Child*, 2002, p. 31, citing Report on the eighth session of the Committee on the Rights of the Child, January 1995, CRC/C/38, p. 3.

48 UNICEF, *Implementation Handbook for the Convention on the Rights of the Child*, 2002, pp. 525, 527.

49 These obligations have been supplemented for those states that are parties to the Optional Protocol to the Convention on the Rights of the Child on the involvement of children in armed conflict.

50 UNICEF, *Implementation Handbook for the Convention on the Rights of the Child*, 2002, p. 563.

51 Concluding Observations of the Committee on the Rights of the Child, Sierra Leone, UN Doc. CRC/C/15/Add.116, 2000, para. 74.

52 Available at http://www.unhchr.ch/html/menu2/6/crc/treaties/opac.htm. This Protocol entered into force on 12 February 2002. It had 88 states parties and 132 signatories on 28 February 2005.

53 Available at http://www.unhchr.ch/html/menu2/6/crc/treaties/opsc.htm. This Protocol entered into force on 18 January 2002. It had 88 state parties and 137 signatories on 28 February 2005.

54 UNICEF has stressed that "the children concerned be treated humanely, with a view to their social rehabilitation". UNICEF, *Implementation Handbook for the Convention on the Rights of the Child*, 2002, p. 647.

55 Available at http://www.unhchr.ch/html/menu3/b/a_ccpr.htm. Entered into force 23 March 1976. It had 153 states parties on 27 October 2004.

56 Human Rights Committee, General Comment No. 31, The Nature of the General Legal Obligation Imposed on States Parties to the Covenant, (Article 2), UN Doc. CCPR/C/21/Rev.1/Add. 13, /2004, para 8. Available at http://www.unhchr.ch/tbs/doc.nsf/(Symbol)/CCPR.C.21.Rev.1.Add.13.En?Opendocument.

57 See *Making rights a reality: The duty of states to address violence against women* (AI Index: ACT 77/049/2004).

58 Human Rights Committee, General Comment No. 28, Equality of rights between men and women, (Article 3), para. 5. Available at www.unhchr.ch/tbs/doc.nsf/(Symbol)/13b02776122d4838802568b900360e80?Opendocument.

59 Human Rights Committee, General Comment No. 28, Equality of rights between men and women (Article 3), 2000, para. 8.

60 Legality of the Threat or Use of Nuclear Weapons, International Court of Justice (Advisory Opinion), 1996 ICJ 226, 1996, para. 25.

61 Legality of the Threat or Use of Nuclear Weapons, International Court of Justice (Advisory Opinion), 1996 ICJ 226, 1996, para. 25.

62 Human Rights Committee, General Comment No. 5, Derogation of Rights (Article 4), 1981, para. 3. Available at http://www.unhchr.ch/tbs/doc.nsf/(Symbol)/ecb5519dedd9b550c12563ed0046d1a1?Opendocument.

63 Human Rights Committee, General Comment No. 29, States of Emergency (Article 4), UN Doc. CCPR/C/21/Rev.1/Add.11, 2001, para. 3. Available at: http://www.unhchr.ch/tbs/doc.nsf/(Symbol)/71eba4be3974b4f7c1256ae200517361?Opendocument.

64 Human Rights Committee, General Comment No. 29, States of Emergency (Article 4), para. 9.

65 Human Rights Committee, General Comment No. 29, States of Emergency (Article 4), para. 16.

66 Human Rights Committee, General Comment No. 29, States of Emergency (Article 4), para. 13.

67 Human Rights Committee, General Comment No. 29, States of Emergency (Article 4), paras. 14 and 15.

68 Human Rights Committee, General Comment No. 28, Equality of Rights between men and women (Article 3), para. 7.

69 Human Rights Committee, General Comment No. 28, Equality of Rights between men and women (Article 3), para. 7.

70 This section is adapted from Bennoune, Karima, "Towards a Human Rights Approach to Armed Conflict: Iraq 2003", 11 *University of California Davis Journal of International Law & Policy*, pp 202-205, Fall 2004. The article contains further discussion of issues related to applying international human rights law in armed conflict, such as the *lex specialis* problem.

71 Manfred Nowak, *UN Covenant on Civil and Political Rights*, CCPR Comment, Engel, 1993, p. 41.

72 Manfred Nowak, *UN Covenant on Civil and Political Rights*, CCPR Comment, Engel, 1993, p. 42.

73 *Lopez v. Uruguay*, Uruguay Communication No. 52/1979, UN Doc:CCPR/C/13/D/52/1979, 7 July 1981, cited in Manfred

Endnotes

Nowak, *UN Covenant on Civil and Political Rights, CCPR Comment*, Engel, 1993, p. 43.

74 *Celiberti* case, Communication No. 56/1979, para. 10(3).

75 *Celiberti* case, Communication No. 56/1979, para. 10(3).

76 Human Rights Committee, General Comment No. 31, The Nature of the General Legal Obligation Imposed on States Parties to the Covenant (Article 2), UN Doc. CCPR/C/21/Rev.1/Add. 13, 2004.

77 Human Rights Committee, General Comment No. 31, The Nature of the General Legal Obligation Imposed on States Parties to the Covenant (Article 2), para. 10.

78 Human Rights Committee, General Comment No. 31, The Nature of the General Legal Obligation Imposed on States Parties to the Covenant, (Article 2), para. 10.

79 Available at http://www.unhchr.ch/html/menu3/b/a_cescr.htm. Entered into force 2 January 1976. It had 150 states parties on 27 October 2004.

80 Committee on Economic, Social and Cultural Rights, General Comment No. 8, The relationship between economic sanctions and respect for economic, social and cultural rights, UN Doc. No. E/C.12/1997/8, 1997.

81 Available at http://www.ohchr.org/english/law/cat.htm. Entered into force 26 June 1987. It had 138 state parties on 27 October 2004.

82 Amnesty International has affirmed in the past that: "Under customary international law, many acts of violence against women committed by parties to a conflict (whether international or internal) constitute torture. These include rape and gang rape, abduction and sexual slavery, forced marriage, forced impregnation and forced maternity, sexual mutilation, indecent assault and many other forms of physical violence." *Broken bodies, shattered minds: Torture and ill-treatment of women* (AI Index: ACT 40/001/2001), p. 54.

83 The inference is that such violence meets all requirements of the definition of torture, including a prohibited purpose such as discrimination or punishment. See, for example, Report of the Special Rapporteur on violence against women, its causes and consequences, UN Doc. E/CN.4/1996/53, paras. 42-50.

84 Available at: http://www.ohchr.org/english/law/cerd.htm. Entered into force 4 January 1969. It had 170 state parties on 27 October 2004.

85 Available at: http://www.unhchr.ch/html/menu3/b/p_genoci.htm. Entered into force 12 January 1951. It had 136 state parties on 27 October 2004.

86 The International Criminal Tribunal for Rwanda in the *Akayesu* case noted that particular prohibited steps include sexual mutilation, sterilization, forced birth control, separation of the sexes and prohibition of marriages. *Prosecutor v. Jean-Paul Akayesu*, Trial Chamber, International Criminal Tribunal for Rwanda (ICTR), 1998, Case No. ICTR-96-4-T; opinion available at http://www.ictr.org/ENGLISH/cases/Akayesu/judgement/akay001.htm, para. 507.

87 *Prosecutor v. Akayesu*, Trial Chamber, International Criminal Tribunal for Rwanda, 1998, Case No. ICTR-96-4-T, paras. 507, 508.

88 Beijing Declaration and Platform for Action, adopted by the Fourth World Conference on Women, 15 September 1995, para. 131. Available at http://www.unesco.org/education/information/nfsunesco/pdf/BEIJIN_E.PDF.

89 ICRC, *Women and War: Special Brochure*, 1995, p. 7.

90 Articles 1(3); 13(1)(b); and 55(c) of the Charter of the United Nations (1945). For text see, for instance, http://www.unhchr.ch/html/menu3/b/ch-cont.htm.

91 Universal Declaration of Human Rights, adopted and proclaimed by General Assembly resolution 217 A (III) of 10 December 1948. Available at: http://www.unhchr.ch/udhr/index.htm.

92 See *Making rights a reality: The duty of states to address violence against women*, Amnesty International (AI Index: ACT 77/049/2004).

93 See, for example Rehn, Elisabeth, and Sirleaf, Ellen J., *Women, War, Peace, The Independent Experts' Assessment of the Impact of Armed Conflict on Women and Women's Role in Peace-building*, UNIFEM, 2002, p. 13. The Committee on the Rights of the Child has also made reference to the fact that "the traditional inferiority affecting girls' lives is seriously aggravated (during time of armed conflict and emergency)." Report on the eighth session of the Committee on the Rights of the Child, UN Doc. CRC/C/38, 1995, pp. 47-52.

94 The Beijing Platform for Action points out, for example, that "women and girls are particularly affected (by violence in armed conflict) because of their status in society and their sex." (para. 135) Beijing Declaration and Platform for Action, adopted by the Fourth World Conference on Women, 15 September 1995. Available at http://www.unesco.org/education/information/nfsunesco/pdf/BEIJIN_E.PDF.

95 Available at: http://www.ohchr.org/english/law/cmw.htm. Entered into force 1 July 2003.

96 Proclaimed by General Assembly resolution 36/55 of 25 November 1981. Available at http://www.ohchr.org/english/law/religion.htm.

97 Human Rights Committee, General Comment No. 6: The right to life (Article 6), 1982, para. 2.

98 See Gowlland-Debbas, Vera, "The Right to Life and Genocide: The Court and an International Public Policy," in Boisson de Chazournes, Laurence, and Sands, Philippe, *International Law, The International Court of Justice and Nuclear Weapons*, Cambridge University Press, 1999, pp. 322-330.

99 See Bennoune, Karima, "Toward a Human Rights Approach to Armed Conflict: Iraq 2003," 11 *University of California-Davis Journal of International Law and Policy*, 2004, pp. 169-226.

100 The list of prohibited purposes provided in Article 1 of the UN Convention against Torture is illustrative, not exhaustive.

101 UN Body of Principles for the Protection of All Persons under Any Form of Detention or Imprisonment, adopted by

the UN General Assembly in resolution 43/173 of 9
December 1988. The quoted text is in footnote 1 to the Body
of Principles which elaborates on Principle 6's prohibition of
torture or other cruel, inhuman or degrading treatment or
punishment.

102 UN Convention against Torture, Article 2(2) (emphasis added).

103 *Broken bodies, shattered minds: Torture and ill-treatment of women*,
Amnesty International (AI Index: ACT 40/001/2001), p. 54.

104 See discussion of CEDAW Committee General
Recommendation 19, in Chapter 5 above.

105 See 1992 oral introduction to report by the Special Rapporteur
on torture to the Commission on Human Rights, UN Doc.
E/CN.4/1992/SR.21, para. 35. This was cited approvingly by the
next Rapporteur, Nigel Rodley, in Report of the Special
Rapporteur submitted pursuant to Commission on Human Rights
resolution 1992/32, UN Doc. E/CN.4/1995/34, 1995, para. 16.

106 See for instance the following cases: *Prosecutor v. Jean-Paul
Akayesu*, Case No. ICTR-96-4-T, ICTR Chamber I, judgment of
2 September 1998, paras. 597, 687; *Prosecutor v. Zejnil Delalic*, Case
No. IT-96-21, ICTY Trial Chamber II, judgment of 16
November 1998, discussion, paras. 475-496, and findings, paras.
943, 965; *Prosecutor v. Anto Furundzija*, Case No. IT-95-17/1-T,
ICTY Trial Chamber II, judgment of 10 December 1998, paras.
264-9; *Fernando and Raquel Mejia v. Peru*, Inter-American
Commission on Human Rights, Report No. 5/96, Case No.
10.970, 1 March 1996, para. B(3)(a); *Aydin v. Turkey*
(57/1996/676/866), European Court of Human Rights,
judgment of 25 September 1997, paras. 13, 20, 86.

107 *Prosecutor v. Jean-Paul Akayesu*, Case No. ICTR-96-4-T, ICTR
Chamber I, judgment of 2 September 1998, para. 691.

108 See *Making rights a reality: The duty of states to address violence
against women*, Amnesty International:(AI Index: ACT
77/049/2004).

109 In the words of the Human Rights Committee: *"The
Committee... observes that the assessment of what constitutes inhuman or
degrading treatment falling within the meaning of article 7 [of the
ICCPR] depends on all the circumstances of the case, such as the duration
and manner or the treatment, its physical or mental effects as well as the
sex, age and state of health of the victim." Antti Vuolanne v. Finland*,
Communication No. 265/1987, (7 April 1989), UN GAOR Sup.
No. 40 (A/44/40), 1989, para 9.2. None of the acts described or
discussed in this report falls below that lower threshold.

110 See Article 16 of the UN Convention against Torture.

111 See Gallagher, Anne, "Human Rights and the New UN
Protocols on Trafficking and Migrant Smuggling: A Preliminary
Analysis", in 23 *Human Rights Quarterly* 4, 2001, for more
information.

112 United Nations Office on Drugs and Crime, What if the
Victim Consents?: More About Trafficking in Human Beings,
2003. Available at
http://www.unodc.org/unodc/trafficking_victim_consents.html, p. 2.

113 Protocol to Prevent, Suppress and Punish Trafficking in
Persons, Especially Women and Children, Supplementing the

United Nations Convention against Transnational Organized
Crime, General Assembly resolution 55/25, annex II, p. 31.
Available at http://daccessdds.un.org/doc/UNDOC/GEN/
N00/560/89/PDF/N0056089.pdf?OpenElement.
The travaux préparatoires, or drafting notes for this Protocol,
UN Doc. A/55/383/Add.1, which may assist in its interpretation,
are available at: http://www.uncjin.org/Documents/Conventions/
dcatoc/final_documents/383a1e.pdf.

114 International Human Rights Law Group, *The Annotated Guide
to the Complete UN Trafficking Protocol*, 2002, p. 2.

115 International Human Rights Law Group, *The Annotated Guide
to the Complete UN Trafficking Protocol*, 2002, p. 3.

116 Note that the consent of the victim is irrelevant under the
Protocol where any of the means listed in Article 3(a) have been
employed. (Article 3(b)). Furthermore, recruitment, transport,
transfer, harbouring or receipt of children for the purposes of
exploitation, even without any of the listed means, constitute
trafficking (Article 3(c)).

117 Exploitation for these purposes includes: the exploitation of
the prostitution of others, forced labour or services, slavery or
servitude or analogous practices or the removal of organs.
(Article 3(a))

118 See Report of the UN High Commissioner for Human
Rights to the Economic and Social Council, UN Doc.
E/2002/68/Add.1, 2002. Available at
http://documents-dds-ny.un.org/doc/UNDOC/GEN/N02/
401/68/pdf/N0240168.pdf?OpenElement.

119 Systematic rape, sexual slavery and slavery-like practices
during armed conflicts, Report of the United Nations High
Commissioner for Human Rights, UN Doc.
E/CN.4/Sub.2/2004/35, 2004, para. 44.

120 Systematic rape, sexual slavery and slavery-like practices
during armed conflict, Update to the final report submitted by
Ms. Gay McDougall, UN Doc. E/CN.4/Sub.2/2000/21, 2000,
paras. 10, 16.

121 Systematic rape, sexual slavery and slavery-like practices
during armed conflict, Update to the final report submitted by
Ms. Gay McDougall, UN Doc. E/CN.4/Sub.2/2000/21, 2000,
para. 8.

122 Systematic rape, sexual slavery and slavery-like practices
during armed conflict, Update to the final report submitted by
Ms. Gay McDougall, UN Doc. E/CN.4/Sub.2/2000/21, 2000,
para. 47.

123 Numerous provisions of contemporary international human
rights law ban slavery. See for example, ICCPR Articles 8(1) and
8(2) which are non-derogable.

124 Cited in Systematic rape, sexual slavery and slavery-like
practices during armed conflict, Update to the final report
submitted by Ms. Gay McDougall, UN Doc.
E/CN.4/Sub.2/2000/21, 2000, para. 21.

125 See Systematic rape, sexual slavery and slavery-like practices,
Sub-Commission on Human Rights resolution 2002/29, UN
Doc. E/CN.4/2003/2, para. 3.

Endnotes

126 Systematic rape, sexual slavery and slavery-like practices during armed conflict, Report of the United Nations High Commissioner for Human Rights, UN Doc. E/CN.4/Sub.2/2004/35, 2004, para. 41.

127 Systematic rape, sexual slavery and slavery-like practices during armed conflict, Update to the final report submitted by Ms. Gay McDougall, UN Doc. E/CN.4/Sub.2/2000/21, 2000, paras. 80-88.

128 Systematic rape, sexual slavery and slavery-like practices during armed conflict, Update to the final report submitted by Ms. Gay McDougall, UN Doc. E/CN.4/Sub.2/2000/21, 2000, para. 51, footnote 61.

129 Sub-Commission on Human Rights resolution 2002/29, para. 5.

130 See, for example, Gardam, Judith, and Jarvis, Michelle, *Women, Armed Conflict and International Law*, Kluwer Law International, 2001, p. 25, footnote 40.

131 Final Report of the Commission of Experts Established Pursuant to Security Council Resolution 780 1992, UN Doc. S/1994/674. See, in particular, the annexes thereto, in UN Doc. S/1994/674/Add.2 (Annexes IX, IX.A and IX.B). These materials are discussed in Gardam, Judith, and Jarvis, Michelle, *Women, Armed Conflict and International Law*, Kluwer Law International, 2001, pp. 148-149.

132 See Women's Initiatives for Gender Justice, *The Crime of Forced Pregnancy*, available at http://www.iccwomen.org/archive/icc/iccpc/rome/forcedpreg.htm.

133 Available at http://www.oas.org/juridico/english/Treaties/a-61.htm.

134 For full ratifications list in English, see http://www.oas.org/juridico/english/Sigs/a-61.html. Last checked 27 October 2004.

135 Protocol to the African Charter on Human and Peoples' Rights on the Rights of Women in Africa, adopted 11 July 2003, available at http://www.africa-union.org/home/Welcome.htm.

136 As of 19 February 2005, only Comoros, Djibouti, Lesotho, Libya, Mali, Namibia, Rwanda, Senegal and South Africa had ratified the Protocol; 27 other countries had signed the Protocol. Updated ratification information is available at http://www.africa-union.org/home/Welcome.htm.

137 Human Rights Education Associates (HREA), *Equality Now, African Union Adopts Protocol on the Rights of African Women: Right to Abortion Articulated For the First Time in International Law*, 2003.

138 Proclaimed by General Assembly resolution 3318(XXIX) of 14 December 1974. Available at http://www.unhchr.ch/html/menu3/b/24.htm.

139 Gardam, Judith, and Jarvis, Michelle, *Women, Armed Conflict and International Law*, Kluwer Law International, 2001, p. 139.

140 Declaration on the Elimination of Violence against Women, General Assembly resolution 48/104 of 20 December 1993. This resolution was adopted by the General Assembly without a vote. Available at http://www.unhchr.ch/huridocda/huridoca.nsf/(Symbol)/A.RES.48.104.En?Opendocument.

141 Beijing Declaration and Platform for Action, adopted by the Fourth World Conference on Women, 15 September 1995. Available at http://www.un.org/womenwatch/daw/beijing/platform/index.html.

142 See discussion in Gardam, Judith, and Jarvis, Michelle, "Women and Armed Conflict: The International Response to the Beijing Platform for Action", 32 *Columbia Human Rights Law Review* 1, 2000, 12-14, p. 55.

143 UN General Assembly resolution 56/132, 19 December 2001, Follow-up to the Fourth World Conference on Women and full implementation of the Beijing Declaration and Platform for Action and the outcome of the twenty-third special session of the General Assembly. This resolution was adopted without a vote.

144 UN Security Council resolution 1325 on Women and Peace and Security, adopted 31 October 2000. UN Doc. S/RES/1325, 2000. Available at http://www.un.org/News/Press/docs/2001/SC6988.doc.htm.

145 Adopted and proclaimed by General Assembly resolution 217 A (III) of 10 December 1948. Available at http://www.un.org/Overview/rights.html.

146 Available at http://www.unhchr.ch/huridocda/huridoca.nsf/(Symbol)/A.CONF.157.23.En?OpenDocument.

147 Adopted by consensus by the 179 states which participated in the International Conference on Population and Development in Cairo, September 1994. For text, as well as declarations and reservations by some states see http://www.unfpa.org/icpd/icpd_poa.htm.

148 For text, see http://www.unhchr.ch/pdf/Durban.pdf.

149 Adopted by resolution 34/169, adopted by the UN General Assembly on 17 December 1979. Available at http://www.ohchr.org/english/law/codeofconduct.htm.

150 Adopted by UN General Assembly resolution 40/34 of 29 November 1985. Available at http://www.ohchr.org/english/law/victims.htm.

151 Rehn, Elisabeth, and Sirleaf, Ellen J., *Women, War, Peace, The Independent Experts' Assessment on the Impact of Armed Conflict on Women and Women's Role in Peace-building*, UNIFEM, 2002.

152 Rehn, Elisabeth, and Sirleaf, Ellen J., *Women, War, Peace, The Independent Experts' Assessment of the Impact of Armed Conflict on Women and Women's Role in Peace-building*, UNIFEM, 2002, p. 19.

153 UN Secretary-General's Bulletin, UN Doc. ST/SGB/2003/13.

154 Available at http://www.reliefweb.int/library/GHRkit/FilesFeb2001.

155 Adopted on 12 August 1949 by the Diplomatic Conference for the Establishment of International Conventions for the Protection of Victims of War, held in Geneva from 12 April to 12 August 1949 (Geneva Conference). Available at http://www.unhchr.ch/html/menu3/b/q_genev1.htm.

156 Adopted on 12 August 1949 by the Geneva Conference. Available at http://www.unhchr.ch/html/menu3/b/q_genev2.htm.

157 Adopted on 12 August 1949 by the Geneva Conference. Available at http://www.unhchr.ch/html/menu3/b/91.htm.

158 Adopted on 12 August 1949 by the Geneva Conference.

Endnotes

Available at http://www.unhchr.ch/html/menu3/b/92.htm.

159 For the updated list of states parties to the conventions and protocols, see http://www.icrc.org/eng/party_gc. Last checked 21 February 2005.

160 Adopted on 8 June 1977 by the Diplomatic Conference on the Reaffirmation and Development of International Humanitarian Law applicable in Armed Conflicts, entered into force 7 December 1978. Available at http://www.unhchr.ch/html/menu3/b/93.htm.

161 As of 21 February 2005.

162 Adopted on 8 June 1977 by the Diplomatic Conference on the Reaffirmation and Development of International Humanitarian Law applicable in Armed Conflicts, entered into force 7 December 1978. Available at http:// www.unhchr.ch/html/menu3/b/94.htm.

163 For more general information on international humanitarian law, see Fleck, D. (ed.), *Handbook of Humanitarian Law in Armed Conflict*, Oxford University Press, 1995.

164 As of 21 February 2005..

165 For more information, see Henckaerts, Jean-Marie and Doswald-Beck, Louise, *Customary International Humanitarian Law*, Cambridge University Press, 2005.

166 On this issue see, for instance, Meron, Theodor, *Human Rights and Humanitarian Norms as Customary Law*, Oxford, Clarendon, 1991, Chapter 1.

167 See, for instance, Ticehurst, Rupert, "The Martens Clause and the Laws of Armed Conflict," *International Review of the Red Cross*, no. 317 (1997), pp. 125-134.

168 See Geneva I, Article 63; Geneva II, Article 62; Geneva III, Article 142; Geneva IV, Article 158; and similarly Protocol I Article 1(2), Protocol II, Preamble.

169 See Article 2, common to the Four Geneva Conventions of 1949; Protocol 1, Article 3.

170 Geneva IV, Article 6, stipulates that this Convention applies "from the outset of any conflict or occupation" covered by the treaty and ceases "on the general close of military operations". In occupied territory, under Geneva IV, the law continues to apply until "one year after the general close of military operations". However, states parties continue to be bound by certain specified obligations even thereafter. It must not be forgotten that some Geneva provisions, such as those on publicizing the Conventions, apply in peacetime as well.

171 Protocol I, Article 3 sets out that this framework applies from the beginning of any of the covered situations through to "the general close of military operations," except in occupied territories where it ceases "on the termination of the occupation, except, in either circumstance, for those persons whose final release, repatriation or re-establishment takes place thereafter". Such persons benefit from the Conventions as long as they have such status.

172 Protocol II, Article 2(2).

173 Common Article 1 has been described as providing "the nucleus for a system of collective responsibility." Boisson de Chazournes,

Laurence, and Condorelli, Luigi, "Common Article 1 of the Geneva Conventions revisited: Protecting collective interests," *International Review of the Red Cross*, No. 837, pp. 67-87. Available at http://www.icrc.org/ web/eng/siteeng0.nsf/htmlall/review?OpenDocument.

174 ICRC Commentary on General Provisions, p. 24. The Commentary provides the ICRC's authoritative, although perhaps by now, on occasion, somewhat outdated interpretation of the Conventions. Available at http://www.icrc.org/ihl.nsf/WebCOMART?OpenView.

175 ICRC Commentary on common Article 1, p. 25.

170 Boisson de Chazournes, Laurence and Condorelli, Luigi, "Common Article 1 of the Geneva Conventions revisited: Protecting collective interests", *International Review of the Red Cross*, No. 837, p. 68.

177 Case Concerning Military and Paramilitary Activities in and against Nicaragua (*Nicaragua v. United States of America*) (Merits), International Court of Justice, Rep. 1986 14, para. 220.

178 See ICRC Commentary, Geneva II, Article 12, para. 4, p. 92.

179 ICRC, *Women and War: Special Brochure*, 1995, p. 6; and Krill, Françoise, "The Protection of Women in International Humanitarian Law", *International Review of the Red Cross*, 1985, No. 249, p. 359. Françoise Krill estimates that 40 provisions are "of specific concern to women".

180 Gardam, Judith, and Jarvis, Michelle, *Women, Armed Conflict and International Law*, Kluwer Law International, 2001, p. 61.

181 Gardam, Judith, and Jarvis, Michelle, *Women, Armed Conflict and International Law*, Kluwer Law International, 2001, p. 61. This is confirmed in Krill, Françoise, "The Protection of Women in International Humanitarian Law", *International Review of the Red Cross*, 1985, No. 249, p. 339.

182 Commentary, Geneva IV, Article 27, para. 3. "Protected persons" are defined, in Article 4, as "those who, at a given moment and in any manner whatsoever, find themselves, in case of a conflict or occupation, in the hands of a Party to the conflict or Occupying Power of which they are not nationals."

183 Case Concerning Military and Paramilitary Activities in and against Nicaragua (*Nicaragua v. United States of America*) (Merits), International Court of Justice, Rep. 1986 14, para. 218.

184 Case Concerning Military and Paramilitary Activities in and against Nicaragua (*Nicaragua v. United States of America*) (Merits), International Court of Justice, Rep. 1986 14, para. 218.

185 *Prosecutor v. Dusko Tadić*, Trial Chamber II, Opinion and judgment of 7 May 1997, para. 559. See also paras. 607, 613-615.

186 Gardam, Judith, and Jarvis, Michelle, *Women, Armed Conflict and International Law*, Kluwer Law International, 2001, p. 63. As Françoise Krill notes, the particular regard is not defined. Krill, Françoise, "The Protection of Women in International Humanitarian Law", *International Review of the Red Cross*, 1985, No. 249, p. 340.

187 Gardam, Judith, and Jarvis, Michelle, *Women, Armed Conflict and International Law*, Kluwer Law International, 2001, p. 63.

188 ICRC Commentary, Geneva II, Article 12, para. 4, p. 92.

189 ICRC Commentary, Geneva II, Article 12, para. 4, p. 92.

190 Gardam, Judith and Jarvis, Michelle, *Women, Armed Conflict and International Law*, Kluwer Law International, 2001, pp. 62-63, 95.

191 ICRC Commentary, Geneva III, Article 14, para. 2, p. 147.

192 ICRC Commentary, Geneva III, Article 14, para. 2, p. 147.

193 ICRC Commentary, Geneva IV, Article 27, para. 2, p. 206.

194 Women, just like men, may be prisoners of war, if they meet the criteria of Geneva III, Article 4, or Protocol 1, Articles 43 and 44, where those standards apply. This category includes members of the armed forces, militia members, and even, subject to certain qualifications, members of "organized resistance movements" who fall into the hands of an adverse power. Prisoners of war qualify for sophisticated layers of protection, found especially throughout Geneva III and in Protocol 1, Articles 43-45 in particular. On the other hand, Geneva IV allows parties to a conflict, only if absolutely necessary for "imperative reasons of security," to confine or intern certain non-combatants without charge or trial, subject to court review. Such internees benefit from numerous provisions of Geneva IV, including Articles 41-43, 68, 78-141. Still other women may find themselves detained subject to criminal charge in conflict situations. They too are protected by a range of provisions of Geneva law.

195 Françoise Krill indicates that Article 14(2) of Geneva III implies that "the separation must be effective, in other words that male prisoners must not have access to the dormitories of women prisoners whether or not the women consent." Krill, Françoise, "The Protection of Women in International Humanitarian Law", *International Review of the Red Cross*, 1985, No. 249, p. 354. Furthermore, it is the responsibility of the Detaining Power to ensure this separation, which, it should be noted, only explicitly refers to dormitories and conveniences; quarters as a whole do not have to be separated.

196 ICRC, *Women and War: Special Brochure*, p. 11. But also see the discussion of this issue in Françoise Krill's article, p. 340.

197 Krill, Françoise, "The Protection of Women in International Humanitarian Law", *International Review of the Red Cross*, 1985, No. 249, p. 348.

198 ICRC commentary, Geneva IV, Article 38, E. "Preferential treatment", pp. 248-249.

199 Beijing Declaration and Platform for Action, para. 133.

200 Gardam, Judith, and Jarvis, Michelle, *Women, Armed Conflict and International Law*, Kluwer Law International, 2001, p. 68. For more information about non-combatant immunity, see Gardam, Judith, *Non-combatant immunity as a norm of international humanitarian law*, Martinus Nijhoff Publishers, 1993.

201 Gardam, Judith, and Jarvis, Michelle, *Women, Armed Conflict and International Law*, Kluwer Law International, 2001, p. 71.

202 In the words of the International Court of Justice: "the minimum rules applicable to international and to non-international conflicts are identical". Case Concerning Military and Paramilitary Activities in and against Nicaragua (*Nicaragua v. United States of America*) (Merits), International Court of Justice Rep. 1986 14, para. 219.

203 This obligation is to be found in Geneva I, Article 49; Geneva II, Article 50; Geneva III, Article 129; Geneva IV, Article 146; and Protocol 1, Article 85 (1) (by implication).

204 Draper, G., "The Modern Pattern of War Criminality", in Dinstein, Y. and Tabory, M. (eds.), *War Crimes in International Law*, 1996, p. 156.

205 See for example Zegveld, Liesbeth , *The Accountability of Armed Opposition Groups in International Law*, Cambridge University Press, 2002, pp. 9-10.

206 Case Concerning Military and Paramilitary Activities in and against Nicaragua (*Nicaragua v. United States of America*) (Merits), ICJ, Rep. 1986 14, para. 116, where the Court takes it for granted that an armed opposition group (the Contras), is capable of committing "violations of humanitarian law".

207 Inter-American Commission on Human Rights, Report No. 55/97, Case No 11.137, *Juan Carlos Abella (Argentina)*, 30 October 1997, para. 174 (known as *Tablada*).

208 Inter-American Commission on Human Rights, Report No. 55/97, Case No 11.137, *Juan Carlos Abella (Argentina)*, 30 October 1997, para. 174.

209 See for example, Commission on Human Rights resolution 2002/14, 19 April 2002, Situation of human rights in the Democratic Republic of the Congo, UN Doc. E/CN.4/2002/200, p. 75, para. 3(b), urging "all parties to the continuing conflict" to protect human rights and respect international humanitarian law, "as applicable to them", including the Additional Protocols.

210 Zegveld, Liesbeth, *The Accountability of Armed Opposition Groups in International Law*, Cambridge University Press, 2002, p. 14.

211 Additional Protocol I, Article 1(4).

212 Additional Protocol I, Article 96(3).

213 *Instructions for the Government of Armies of the United States in the Field*, was prepared by Francis Lieber, LL.D. in 1863, during the Civil War in the USA, and was published by order of the Secretary of War. Known as the Lieber Code, many of its provisions have passed into customary international law.

214 The Commission of Responsibilities of the Authors of the War and the Enforcement of Penalties was established by the victorious allies in 1919 to bring to justice those responsible for the First World War and for crimes perpetrated (by the losing states) during the war.

215 Control Council Law No. 10, Punishment of Persons Guilty of War Crimes, Crimes Against Peace and Against Humanity, 20 December 1945, Article II(1)(a).

216 Convention (IV) respecting the Laws and Customs of War on Land and its annex: Regulations concerning the Laws and Customs of War on Land. The Hague, 18 October 1907, Article 46.

217 See for example, Transcript of Oral Judgment, Women's International War Crimes Tribunal (Tokyo Tribunal) on Japan's Military Sexual Slavery, para. 6. See http://www.iccwomen.org/tokyo/summary.htm.

218 Adapted from, "Treatment of Sexual Violence in International Law," available at http://www.iccwomen.org/resources/crimeschart.htm.

219 For further discussion of jurisprudence in the area of ad hoc international criminal tribunals, see Askin, Kelly, *War Crimes Against Women: Prosecution in International War Crimes Tribunals*, Martinus Nijhoff, 1997.

220 Adapted from, "Treatment of Sexual Violence in International Law," available at http://www.iccwomen.org/resources/crimeschart.htm.

221 See, for example, *Prosecutor v. Zejnil Delalic*, Case No. IT-96-21, ICTY Trial Chamber II, judgment of 16 November 1998, discussion, paras. 475-496, and findings, paras. 943, 965; *Prosecutor v. Anto Furundzija*, Case No. IT-95-17/1-T, ICTY Trial Chamber, judgment of 10 December 1998, paras. 264-9.

222 See http://www.ictr.org/ENGLISH/basicdocs/statute.html, Article 4(e).

223 *Prosecutor v. Jean-Paul Akayesu*, Case No. ICTR-96-4-T, ICTR Chamber I, judgment of 2 September 1998, para. 597.

224 *Prosecutor v. Jean-Paul Akayesu*, Case No. ICTR-96-4-T, ICTR Chamber I, judgment of 2 September 1998, paras. 507-8.

225 *Prosecutor v. Jean-Paul Akayesu*, Case No. ICTR-96-4-T, judgment of 2 September 1998.

226 *Prosecutor v. Kunarać et al*, Case No. IT-96-23 and IT-96-23/1, ICTY Trial Chamber II, judgment of 22 February 2001.

227 In one case, *Prosecutor v. Tadić*, it permitted the use of anonymous witnesses, which Amnesty International opposes. See *International Criminal Court: Making the right choices – Part II: Organizing the court and ensuring a fair trial*, Amnesty International (AI Index: IOR 40/011/1997).

228 *Prosecutor v. Jean-Paul Akayesu*, Case No. ICTR-96-4-T, ICTR Chamber I, judgment of 2 September 1998, para 598.

229 The *Akayesu* definition of rape, although hailed as a significant advance in 1998, is in some ways more restrictive than the more recent jurisprudence of the International Criminal Tribunal for the former Yugoslavia in the *Kunarać* case (Case No. IT-96-23, Judgment, Appeals Chamber, 12 June 2002.

230 Rome Statue of the International Criminal Court, adopted on 17 July 1998, UN Doc. A/CONF.183/9, entered into force on 1 July 2002. Available at: http://www.un.org/law/icc/statute/romefra.htm. It had 97 states parties and 139 signatories on 29 October 2004.

231 See definition of enslavement in Article 7(2)(c) of the Rome Statute of the International Criminal Court.

232 Article 36 (8) (a) (iii) of the Rome Statute of the International Criminal Court.

233 As of 29 February 2005. Updated ratification information available at http://www.untreaty.un.org/ENGLISH/BIBLE/englishinternetbible/partI/chapterXVIII/treaty10.asp.

234 As of 15 February 2005, the Convention relating to the Status of Refugees and its Protocol had 142 states parties each. Updated ratification information is available at http://www.unhcr.ch.

235 Text available at http://www.ohchr.org/english/law/refugees.htm.

236 The 1967 Protocol removed the requirement that a refugee claim relate to "events occurring in Europe before 1 January 1951".

237 Notwithstanding, UNHCR's mandate, as set out in the Statute of the Office of the UN High Commissioner for Refugees and subsequent resolutions of the UN General Assembly and the UN Economic and Social Council (ECOSOC), covers all persons outside their country of origin for reasons of feared persecution, armed conflict, generalized violence, foreign aggression or other circumstances which have seriously disturbed public order and who, as a result, require international protection.

238 This treaty had 41 state parties as of Februray 2005 . Updated ratification information and text are available at http://www1.umn.edu/humanrts/instree/z2arcon.htm.

239 The Preamble of the Refugee Convention, for example, starts by referring to the principle "that human beings shall enjoy fundamental rights and freedoms without discrimination" as affirmed in the Charter of the UN and the Universal Declaration of Human Rights. It proceeds by considering that the UN has "endeavoured to assure refugees the widest possible exercise of these fundamental rights and freedoms". Such rights would include all the rights in the International Bill of Human Rights.

240 The EXCOM was established by the UN Economic and Social Council (ECOSOC) in 1958, pursuant to General Assembly resolution 1166 (XII). It consists of state representatives elected by ECOSOC and functions as a subsidiary organ of the General Assembly. All EXCOM Conclusions, as well as all other documents referenced in this section, are available at http://www.unhcr.ch.

241 UNHCR EXCOM Conclusion No. 81 (XLVIII) General Conclusion on International Protection, UN Doc. A/AC.96/895, 1997, para. (g).

242 See for example EXCOM Conclusion No. 39 (XXXVI) Refugee Women and International Protection, 1985, paras (c) (d) (e); EXCOM Conclusion No. 54 (XXXIX) Refugee Women, 1988; EXCOM Conclusion No. 60 (XL) Refugee Women, 1989 para (b); EXCOM Conclusion No. 64 (XLI) Refugee Women and International Protection, 1990, para. (a),(v); EXCOM Conclusion No. 68 (XLIII), General Guidelines on International Protection, 1992, para (i); EXCOM Conclusion No. 77 (XLVI) General Guidelines on International Protection, 1995, para (g), EXCOM Conclusion No. 87(L), General Conclusion on International Protection, 1999, para (n).

243 UNHCR, *Guidelines on the Protection of Refugee Women*, 1991.

244 UNHCR, *Sexual and Gender-Based Violence against Refugees, Returnees and Internally Displaced Persons: Guidelines for Prevention and Response*, 2003.

245 UNHCR, *Guidelines on International Protection: Gender-Related Persecution within the context of Article 1A(2) of the 1951 Convention and/or its 1967 Protocol relating to the Status of Refugees*, UN Doc. HCR/GIP/02/01, 2002.

246 WHO, UNFPA and UNHCR, *Inter-agency Field Manual on Reproductive Health in Refugee Situations*, UNHCR, 1999.

247 See UNHCR Mid-Year Progress Report 2002 Global Programmes.

Endnotes

248 UN Doc. E/CN.4/1998/53/Add.2, 1998, available at www.unhchr.ch/html/menu2/7/b/principles.htm.

249 ICRC, *Women and War: Special Brochure*, p. 26. See also, ICRC, Advancement of Women and Implementation of the Outcome of the Fourth World Conference on Women, Statement before the UN General Assembly, 1998. Available at http://www.icrc.org/icrceng.nsf/5cacfdf48ca698b641256242003b 3295/d366866e92d18001412566a4004eb94c?OpenDocument.

250 Krill, Françoise, "The Protection of Women in International Humanitarian Law", *International Review of the Red Cross*, 1985, No. 249, p. 360.

251 For example, see the discussion of the Commentaries above.

252 Gardam, Judith and Jarvis, Michelle, "Women and Armed Conflict: The International Response to the Beijing Platform for Action", 32 *Columbia Human Rights Law Review* 1, 2000, 12-14, p. 56.

253 Gardam, Judith, and Jarvis, Michelle, "Women and Armed Conflict: The International Response to the Beijing Platform for Action", 32 *Columbia Human Rights Law Review* 1, 2000, 12-14, p. 57.

254 Gardam, Judith, and Jarvis, Michelle, offer a model draft of such principles in "Women and Armed Conflict: The International Response to the Beijing Platform for Action", 32 *Columbia Human Rights Law Review* 1, 2000, 12-14, p. 58.

INDEX

K

Kosovo: 44
Krill, Françoise: 51, 67
Kunarac et al case, known as *Foca*: 61

L

law enforcement: 6, 14, 20, 25, 28, 30, 35, 38, 42, 43, 65
Lieber Code: 61
Lopez Burgos case: 19

M

Martens clause: 47
medical experimentation: 4, 17
migrant women: 5, 35
mothers: 4, 5, 19, 29

N

Nicaragua case: 48, 49, 59
non-combatant immunity: 55
non- refoulement: 65
non-state actors (see also armed groups): 12, 17, 24, 40, 65, 68
non-treaty standards: 12, 30, 32
Nowak, Manfred: 19
Nuremberg Tribunal: 61

O

Optional Protocol to CEDAW: 15
Optional Protocol to the Convention on the Rights of the Child on the involvement of children in armed conflict: 9, 16
Optional Protocol to the Convention on the Rights of the Child on the sale of children, child prostitution and child pornography: 17

P

peacekeepers: 5, 6, 25, 44, 45
peacekeeping: 19, 37
poor women: 5
post-conflict situations: 1, 6, 17, 29, 30, 31, 43, 44, 68
pregnant women: 17, 50, 51, 52
principle of distinction: 55
Principles of Medical Ethics Relevant to the Role of Health Personnel, particularly Physicians, in the Protection of Prisoners and Detainees against Torture and Other Cruel, Inhuman or Degrading Treatment or Punishment: 43
Principles on the Effective Investigation and Documentation of Torture and Other Cruel, Inhuman or Degrading Treatment or Punishment: 43
proportionality: 55, 56
prostitution: 3, 4, 14, 35, 37, 44, 51, 53, 62, 66
Protocol Additional to the Geneva Conventions of 12
August 1949, and Relating to the Protection of Victims of International Armed Conflicts (Protocol I): 47, 49, 51, 53, 54, 55, 57, 58, 59
Protocol Additional to the Geneva Conventions of 12 August 1949, and Relating to the Protection of Victims of Non-International Armed Conflicts (Protocol II): 47, 49, 51, 52, 53, 54, 55, 56, 57, 58, 59, 61
Protocol to Prevent, Suppress and Punish Trafficking in Persons, Especially Women and Children: 25, 26

R

rape: 3, 4, 13, 18, 20, 21, 24, 27, 29, 30, 31, 36, 41, 50, 51, 53, 54, 57, 58, 61, 62, 63, 66
refoulement: 65
refugee law: 26
refugees: 4, 5, 6, 8, 10, 16, 25, 29, 31, 33, 35, 37, 38, 64, 65, 66
representation, women: 7, 38, 63
Rehn, Elisabeth: 43
right to peace: 29
right to life: 7, 14, 15, 17, 18, 20, 23, 29, 40

S

Safeguards guaranteeing protection of the rights of those facing the death penalty: 43
sex workers: 5
sexual abuse: 3, 4, 16, 20, 24, 25, 53, 57, 61, 65
sexual assault: 13, 14, 24, 27, 29, 37, 44, 62
sexual humiliation: 4, 61
sexual mutilation: 4, 24, 54, 57
sexual slavery: 4, 24, 26, 27, 30, 31, 33, 34, 37, 57, 58, 61, 62
single mothers: 5
single women: 5
Sirleaf, Ellen: 43
slavery: 17, 18, 24, 26, 27, 40, 54, 62, 66
Special Court for Sierra Leone: 26, 58
Standard Minimum Rules for the Treatment of Prisoners: 43
state of emergency: 7, 18
Sub-Commission on the Promotion and Protection of Human Rights: 26, 27

T

Tablada case: 59
torture: 4, 5, 9, 14, 15, 16, 17, 18, 20, 23, 24, 25, 30, 37, 40, 42, 53, 54, 57, 61, 63, 65, 66
trafficking: 25, 26
trafficking : 44
trafficking in women: 3, 4, 14, 35, 36, 57
treaties: 8, 9, 12, 22, 23, 57, 65

U

UN Charter: 22, 38
UN Commission on Human Rights: 59, 60
UN High Commissioner for Human Rights: 9, 26, 43

Index